The World of Laurel and Hardy

The World of Laurel and Hardy

Thomas Leeflang

Translated by Phil Goddard

WINDWARD

This edition published 1988 by
WINDWARD
an imprint owned by WH Smith & Son Ltd
Registered No. 237811 England Trading as WHS Distributors
St Johns House, East Street, Leicester LE1 6NE

The World of Laurel and Hardy was produced by Bookworld International Ltd for Windward

Design and editorial by Mackenzie Publishing Ltd
Layout and artwork by Keith Smith
Translation by AGET Language Services

First published in the Netherlands as De wereld van Laurel en Hardy by Unieboek B.V. © Unieboek B.V. 1986

ISBN 0711 204 942

Typeset by Keene Graphics, London
Printed in Spain by Artes Graficas Toledo SA.

D. L. TO: 368-1988

And don't call me Ollie!
Oliver Hardy in 'Perfect Day' (1929)

LAUREL
HARDY
USA • TEN CENTS

Contents

Laurel and Hardy are popular worldwide, and many people collect their memorabilia.

KERSTFEEST
met André
A WALTON FILM
A WALTON FILM
A WALTON FILM
A WALTON FILM
A WALTON FILM
A WALTON FILM
A WALTON FILM
WALTON
André van Duin
André Hazes

1

Act One

We all have something of the child in us: we do not simply wake up one day and find we have turned from children into adults. Childhood goes on exercising its influence for the rest of our lives; in many ways we are still children trying to make sense of the adult world.

And it is the child in us which helps us to appreciate the genius of Stan Laurel and Oliver Hardy. Their humour is not the sophisticated, sharp-edged comedy of the 1980s, but it still has something which appeals to a generation reared on the likes of 'Monty Python' and 'Fawlty Towers'. Equally, there are deep-seated reasons why film critics are also taking the comic duo more seriously than ever before.

The reasons for the appeal of Laurel and Hardy are manifold. Firstly, there is the simple fact of their physical *appearance*. Stan Laurel is the nervous, flat-footed, slender underdog who scratches his head on the frequent occasions that he is confused or bewildered by the turn events have taken and whose features dissolve into tears during moments of severe stress. Oliver Hardy is an underdog, too, but he is unaware of the fact. He is fat, pompous and tetchy and constantly aware of his supposed intellectual superiority compared to Stan, fuming at the camera in exasperation at his partner's antics. And yet the two of them stick together through all the adversity that life pushes in their direction, doting on each other with all the devotion of a married couple.

But apart from their appearance, they have another string to their bow: some of the finest *scripts* in the history of comedy, written by themselves and a talented team of writers who included Hiram M. 'Beanie' Walker. All of us, no matter how long ago it may have been since we last watched a Laurel and Hardy film, must surely have a particular gag or scene which remains etched in our minds long after the rest of the film has been forgotten. It may be a street full of people

Big Business, (1929): Laurel and Hardy try to sell James Finlayson a Christmas tree in the middle of summer. The scene ends with the total destruction of Finlayson's house and Laurel and Hardy's car.

hurling pies at each other in *The Battle of the Century* (1927) or the sight of Laurel and Hardy trying to earn a crust as street musicians in a blizzard-swept road in *Below Zero* (1930).

And thirdly, there is the pleasure of *recognition,* that pleasant sense of familiarity we have when a situation we recognize crops up again and again. There is the music which features in so many of their films, the catchy little 'Cuckoo Song' which many people find themselves whistling without any clear idea of its origin. And there are the multitude of Laurel and Hardy trademarks which still somehow manage to be fresh and funny no matter how often they are used: Oliver twiddling his thumbs and his tie in exasperation and nervousness respectively, and Stan 'crying' when he is confused. Equally, the duo managed to get away with using the same stock situations over and over again, such as the 'revenge' scenes where an insult leads to an act of destructive revenge, which itself in turn is revenged, and so on until there is mayhem on a massive scale. An example is the traffic jam in *Two Tars* (1928), which begins with an altercation between Stan and Oliver in one car and Edgar Kennedy in another, and ends with pieces of motor-car strewn across the street.

But far more important than any of these, the essence of Laurel and Hardy's humour is their *innocence.* They are like children, going through life with only semi-comprehension of the strange and upredictable world they live in. When we laugh at them, it is not malicious laughter at someone who is suffering a misfortune but deserves everything he gets: it is the sympathetic laughter accorded to a child who drops an ice-cream. Hal Roach, the owner of the studios where Laurel and Hardy's talents developed and the one man who played the greatest part in their success, said: 'Laughter comes from chidren...as far as people are concerned, the great comedians imitate children...Hardy's action with the tie, Laurel scratching his head – these are actions of a child. Laurel never cried when he was angry, he never cried when he was hurt, he never cried when he was scared. He only cried when he was confused – that's why it's so funny when he cries.'

And this perhaps helps to explain why, although many adults nowadays admire the comic genius of Laurel and Hardy, the pair do not provoke as much hilarity as they used to – except amongst children. It must be easier for a child to identify with these two children in adults' bodies; perhaps more readily with the overt naivety of Stan than with the gruff impatience of Oliver, who is almost a 'big brother' to Stan. To a child who wants to remain a child for the rest of his life, they are a source of comfort, for Stan Laurel and Oliver Hardy have not grown up. Faced with a day out in Atlantic City, Stan packs his toy yacht. In *Brats* (1930), they play both themselves and their own children, and in their very brief appearance in an 'Our Gang' film, *Wild Poses* (1933), they play two babies. Much of their acting is pure pantomime, reflecting Stan Laurel's background on the British stage. For example, the plot of *Babes in Toyland* (1934) has the pair as apprentice toymakers working for Mother Peep and commissioned by Santa Claus to make 600

Night Owls, (1930).

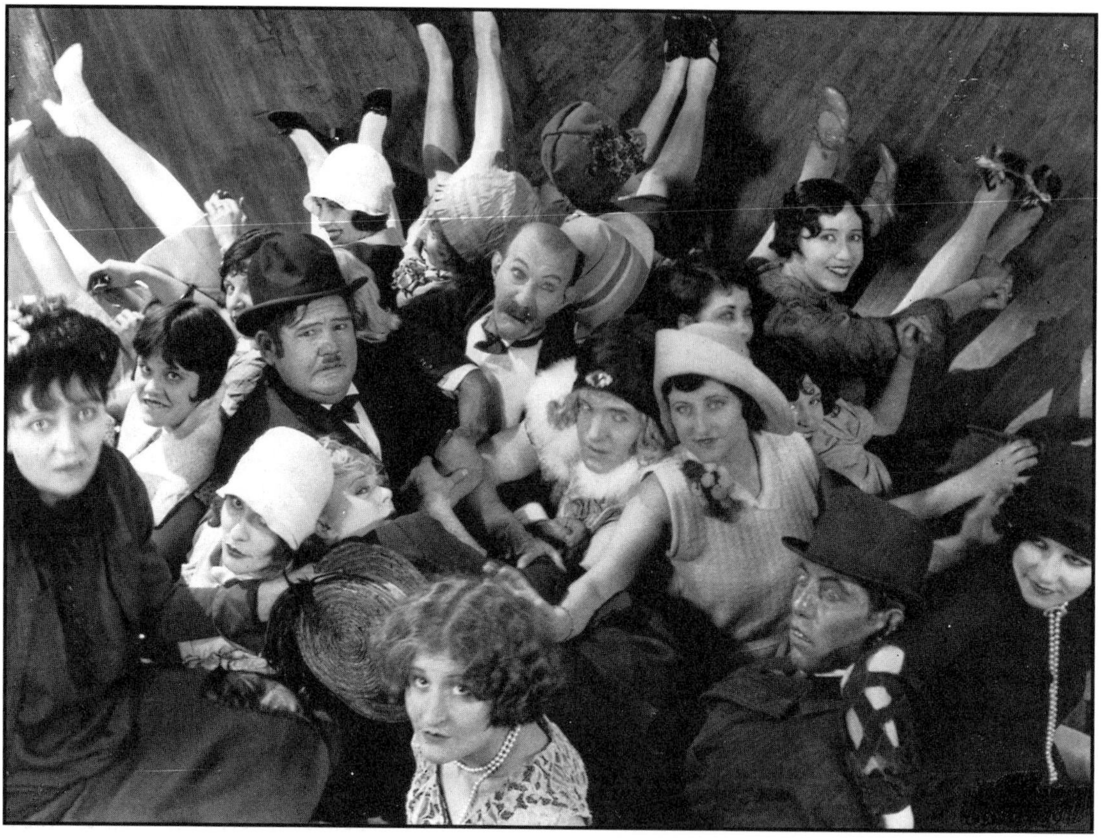

Sugar Daddies, (1927): A Hal Roach film from the All Star Series.

soldiers one foot high – though of course Stan manages to make it 100 soldiers six feet high.

So even though children are often reduced to helpless laughter by the antics of Laurel and Hardy, the duo have a strong and enthusiastic following in the adult world as well, for all of us sometimes have that feeling that we have lost control and nothing we actually do can stem the tide of events that threatens to engulf us. As George Orwell says of Stan, he is 'a less responsible man who is inside of all of us, can never be suppressed altogether, and needs a hearing occasionally'. And although they were spurned by many critics at the time, who placed them in a different league to Charlie Chaplin, Buster Keaton, Harold Lloyd or the Marx Brothers, almost everyone nowadays concurs that they made a great, and unequalled contribution to the history of film comedy. During the fifties and sixties they underwent a major revival as their films began appearing on TV and compilations were made for the cinema of highlights from some of their best movies. The advent of video has brought them to a new audience, who were not brought up on Laurel and Hardy shorts seen at Saturday children's matinées. And there is clearly a gap which is filled by their films. As Hal Roach said of this revival. 'It's because there's a lack of that kind of comedy. People appreciate them more now because they haven't got any competition. Nobody's doing what they did. It seems to me that for the last four or five years people have been laughing at things that aren't funny, just

Leave 'Em Laughing, (1928): Stan and Oliver are overcome by laughing gas after a visit to the dentist.

because they're dying to laugh.'

And although no one could ever accuse Laurel and Hardy of being highbrow, they are being taken seriously by modern critics, for they exercised an influence on drama and film which is only just beginning to be explored. When Harold Pinter and the French New Wave cinema were hailed for their use of the *point mort* – an interval in the film where nothing is actually happening or being said but the pause is sinister, pregnant with meaning – the fact that Laurel and Hardy had been doing the same thing decades previously initially passed unnoticed. And when the tramps in Beckett's *Waiting for Godot* play endlessly with their hats and look inside them as though gaining some kind of reassurance from them in their alien world, Beckett is paying deliberate homage to Laurel and Hardy. In *The Music Box* (1932) the two, who are quasi-tramps themselves, will even interrupt their futile attempts to get a piano up a flight of stairs to retrieve their lost hats and put them on again before they can continue. Laurel and Hardy have the same exaggerated idea of their own importance as the characters in Beckett's play, but any laughter which Beckett's tramps may provoke is of a far different kind to that which Laurel and Hardy arouse. Laurel and Hardy are trying to be something which they are not, affecting a dignity which they do not have. Their dress – stand-up collars, ties, derbies – and their mannerisms – Oliver's malapropisms, his extended little finger when he drinks a cup of tea and his exaggerated gallantry with the opposite sex:

all are designed to create an impression, but it is never long before the balloon of their egos is abruptly deflated. Punctured dignity, the pretensions of humanity being revealed for the sham they are, is a key feature of satire.

The pairing of Laurel and Hardy as a comedy team was almost accidental. Their career together began in 1927, though both of them had long pedigrees in entertainment. It was Hal Roach who saw that the two comedians might be good when working on their own, but could only be great if they worked together. It was Roach who pioneered a new brand of film comedy, exemplified by Harold Lloyd, Charley Chase and 'Our Gang', replacing the fast-paced, manic humour of the Mack Sennett comedies with something much more sedate. In Roach's comedies, the audience actually had time to identify with the characters on the screen, and pauses were used for comic effect, so that one laugh from the audience did not follow too closely on the heels of the last one.

It was Roach, too, who provided the creative atmosphere in which Laurel and Hardy could excel. The Hal Roach Studios may have been a 'fun factory', turning out large volumes of comedies in a short space of time, but there was an air of relaxed hard work and camaraderie which simply did not exist in the larger studios. Making a film was a constant process of dialogue, debate and experiment involving everyone on the studio floor. Many of the films started out from the sketchiest of outlines, and the perfect pacing and humour of the end product often belies the fact that they contain so much improvisation. Although the films were sometimes tried out on audiences to make sure that they fulfilled their quota of seventy-five laughs per two-reel film, the process of making them was anything but mechanical, and Stan Laurel especially was a craftsman who played a major part in the technical side of his films and often stayed on in the editing room long after everyone else had gone home. Frequently, too, the director would happily take a back seat whilst Stan organized the crew the way he wanted them. Said George Douglas, who worked with Laurel and Hardy at the Roach Studios for many years and eventually directed *Saps at Sea*, 'Stan Laurel was the greatest gag man I've ever known – he could think of unbelievably funny business. He would sit in on the cutting, but Stan was always moving on to the next project. He was a tomorrow man rather than a yesterday man. He was working ahead of the clock.' And as a result of the freedom they were given, nearly all their finest films were made for Hal Roach Studios.

Nowhere is this more clearly seen than in the fact that when Laurel and Hardy left Roach in 1941 and went to work for the more prestigious 20th Century-Fox and MGM, many of their creative talents were immediately stifled. No longer were they allowed to play a part in writing their scripts, directing the filming or editing the results – that was all done for them. The films were made for speed and cheapness, capitalizing on the Laurel and Hardy name. And it shows, for inevitably they stopped caring so much about the final result, and their films post-Roach are more insipid, less finely crafted, until towards the end of their

You're Darn Tootin, (1928).

careers some of them are downright bad.

Another important feature of their career together is that it spanned the era of the silent and the sound film. Other comedians – Chaplin and Keaton are the two best examples – did not make the transition successfully because the type of stylized acting required by the silents had become too ingrained in them. But it is to Laurel and Hardy's eternal credit that they excelled both on the silent screen and in the 'talkies'. Both of them were superb pantomime actors who could use their bodies to express a vast range of emotion without once opening their mouths, and it is notable that even the sound films contain long periods where neither of them needs to say anything. But when sound arrived, their audiences found they had voices which exactly fitted their screen personalities: they were even funnier once one could hear what they were saying.

The relationship between the two characters at the outset was a fairly two-dimensional one. Oliver Hardy's background before they started acting together was as a stock 'heavy' character, in mainly serious roles, often a villain – though most people agreed he was one of the best in the business. Stan Laurel was a somewhat manic clown who threw himself around the stage a lot. But the relationship quickly became much more rounded, softening at the edges until the two characters were believable and human. It has often been said that each brought out comic talents in the other which might have remained latent for the rest of the lives had they not played together. And gradually they brought in more of their off-screen personalities, which included playing under their real names, although Oliver's nickname of 'Babe' was never used on screen. Very soon, they were two complex, credible and very funny personalities.

As these personalities grew and became recognized the world over, another element entered into the relationship between them and their audiences. Laurel and Hardy put a great deal of love into their film-making, for comedy was no nine-to-five job. Anyone watching the films could see how much energy had been expended on making sure the finished product was perfect in every detail. From this grew a love of the two actors and their screen personalities, which by now had become inextricably linked, by their audiences. For a long time the two comedians, labouring away in Hollywood, were not fully aware of the emotions they were inspiring amongst their millions of fans in the

Two Tars, (1928).

Two Tars, (1928).

outside world. When the two of them visited Ireland in 1953 for what was to have been a quiet holiday, they were unprepared for the reception that greeted them. Stan recalled later:

> The love and affection we found that day at Cobh was simply unbelievable. There were hundreds of boats blowing whistles, and mobs and mobs of people screaming on the decks. We just couldn't understand what it was all about. And then something happened that I can never forget. All the church bells in Cobh started to ring out our theme song, and Babe looked at me, and we cried. Maybe people loved us and our pictures because we put so much love into them.

Add to this the fact that Stan Laurel, like Charlie Chaplin, was very much a British comedian who had gone to the New World and made good, and the tumultuous welcome they received can be understood.

Half a century has passed since the heyday of Laurel and Hardy, and a generation has grown up in which people no longer revere them on such a grand scale; some, it must be admitted, no longer find them funny any more. But still their films can fill independent cinemas and sell videos, and they still have their fanatical devotees. In 1971 Tom Sefton, President of the San Diego Trust and Savings Bank, confessed to regularly getting out of bed at 3.30 a.m. to watch Laurel and Hardy movies: at least the advent of video means people no longer have to go to such extremes.

Stan Laurel and Oliver Hardy were ordinary, lovable people, both in their films and in their private lives. The characters they played were the kind of people who might well be sitting in the audience – soldiers, sailors, waiters, labourers, travelling salesmen. The situations in the films at least started off as ordinary ones before they degenerated into anarchy and chaos. Although they get a raw deal out of life, they simply shrug their shoulders and get on with the job, taking the good with the bad. Laurel and Hardy are ordinary, lovable people who we can identify with. As John Grierson said of them in the 1930s: 'They are perhaps the Civil Servants of Comedy. No wonder that the life they lead goes to the heart of the multitude.'

S.S. PERIWINKLE
S.S. PERIWINKLE

2

Laurel and Hardy: The faces behind the image

Many a tenacious historian, writer, journalist and student of the cinema has unravelled, analysed and discussed the work of Laurel and Hardy. Innumerable articles, books and television programmes have been written about the two. At the peak of the Laurel and Hardy revival in the early sixties, anyone putting together a television programme made up of extracts from their films had a virtually guaranteed audience. Even now, though their humour may be losing some of its appeal, everyone knows who Stan and Oliver are, knows that they are two funny men and that their humour has a profundity to it which is missing from many modern-day comedians.

And yet the history of cinema comedy is a chaotic muddle of facts, names and film titles, gleaned from books, magazine articles and interviews, and these facts often contradict one another. This is particularly true of Stan Laurel and Oliver Hardy, who were not great self-publicists in the way some of the Hollywood megastars were, and it is no small task to attempt a thorough biography of the two.

This book therefore makes comparatively little mention of the private lives of Stan and Oliver. The first reason is that there are already many publications put together with a great deal of care and affection and unlikely to be surpassed. The subjects of these biographies have both died, and can therefore furnish no more information about themselves, and so have many members of their families and circles of friends and acquaintances. Secondly, comparing information from one source with information from another is a lengthy and dispiriting process: much will never become clear and much is irretrievably lost.

So as not to make this book too chaotic, and to avoid having to refer to the subject later on, a word about their respective personalities away from the cameras seems in order here. Stan appears to have been a

Hog Wild, (1930): the French version, with Yola d'Avril.

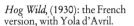

highly principled man who courted the women in his life in honourable fashion and married them all. This naturally affected not only the course of his life, but also the contents of his films and his achievements as an actor. There were four women altogether in Stan's life, and he married officially five times. The women who successively bore the surname Laurel were Lois Nelson, who he married in 1926, Virginia Ruth Rogers, whom he married twice, in 1934 and 1941, Vera Ivanova Shuvalova, supposedly a countess, to whom he was married in 1938, and finally Ida Kitaeva Raphael, a singer born in China of White Russian parents, whom he married in 1946.

Oliver Hardy was married twice: in 1925 to Myrtle Lee Reeves (they were divorced in 1937) and in 1940 to a freelance script clerk, Lucille Jones, who stayed with him for the rest of his life.

Oliver Norvell Hardy's main spare-time occupation was sport, which included an obsession with golf and card-playing and an addiction to betting on horses. In 1933 his first wife Myrtle began pressing for a divorce after Oliver lost $30,000 in one day at the races. Good food, a nice glass of wine and luxurious surroundings, and Oliver was happy.

Of Stan Laurel, it could be said that his main hobby was making films. Often he literally worked day and night, far beyond the scope of his contract, writing and rewriting scripts, and spending long hours in the editing room. This was a fundamental difference between him and Oliver: although Oliver cared just a much that the finished product should be as perfect as possible, his leisure was just as important to him as his work. But Stan Laurel also liked to surround himself with friends, preferably unconnected either with films or the theatre. He liked a glass of whisky, was a great partygoer and had a predilection for sailing as well. One of his friends was Philip K. Wrigley, the chewing-gum king. Wrigley was a man of great wealth and few words: the longest public speech he is ever known to have made was two words: 'Thank you!' Stan Laurel read very little, but when he did open a book it was more often than not about English variety artists such as Little Tich (1868-1928), George Robey (1869-1954), Vesta Tilley (1864-1952) or, above all, Dan Leno (1860-1904), who was once described as the most popular man on the English music-hall stage. One of the tricks Laurel learned from Dan Leno was the idea of saying something perfectly serious and logical, and then repeating it in distorted form for comic effect after Oliver Hardy has asked him to say it again. In *Towed in a Hole* they are fishmongers:

Stan: If we caught our own fish, we wouldn't have to pay for it then. Whoever we sold it to, it would be clear profit.
Oliver: Tell me that again.
Stan: Well if . . . if you caught a fish and whoever you sold it to, they wouldn't have to pay for it. Then we . . . profits would . . . would go to the fish. If . . . If you . . . Pooh!

These were books he had ordered from England, presumably with some difficulty since, compared to the present day, in the 1930s hardly anything had been written about the music hall.

In 1928, Stan's daughter Lois was born. She is now married to a television writer and living in Los Angeles. Stan's son, Stan Junior (Stanley Robert Jefferson), was born two months prematurely on 7 May 1930 and lived for only nine days.

There are a thousand interesting pieces of trivia about Laurel and Hardy's lives outside the film studios which have had to be omitted from this very briefest of outlines. Many of these have never been published, and others appeared in the popular magazines about film stars which sold so well in the thirties and forties (e.g. *Photoplay*, June 1933: 'Stan Laurel: the pathos behind the smile!'), but most of the articles offered no real insight into the lives of Laurel and Hardy, being merely rewrites of press releases from the Publicity Department of

Way Out West, (1936): One of Laurel and Hardy's funniest features, a parody Western.

MGM about Stan's 'marriage scandals' and Oliver's supposedly unquenchable gambling fever. These alternated with the frequently published rumours of a split between Laurel and Hardy, saying they could not stand the sight of each other and could not work together any more. We know now that these rumours were untrue, but of course we have the benefit of hindsight.

Despite the existence of two excellent biographies, *Stan,* by Fred Lawrence Guiles, and *Mr Laurel and Mr Hardy* by John McCabe, little or nothing is known of their private lives. Their lives as children are well documented and illustrated with photographs plundered from the albums of members of the family, but from the moment that they became highly paid film stars and began to live an appropriate lifestyle, Laurel and Hardy managed to keep the press pretty well at bay. Nor was this a particularly difficult thing to do, for although Laurel and Hardy reached a huge audience, they never belonged to the ranks of the Hollywood superstars in the eyes of show-business reporters.

3

Stan Laurel

Stan Laurel was born on 16 June 1890 and christened Arthur Stanley Jefferson. He began life in Ulverston in Lancashire, in the house of his grandmother ('A dear little old lady of fragrant memory' according to his father, Arthur J. Jefferson). Because of his mother's constant illness, Stan was looked after by his grandmother until he was five or six. Eventually he moved to his parents' house in North Shields once his mother, Madge Metcalfe, was able to look after Stan, his sister Olga and brothers Teddy and Gordon. Madge Metcalfe was an actress with the Jefferson Theatre Group, which toured England led by show-business veteran and playwright Arthur J. Jefferson. Stan inherited his father's love of the stage and decided to become an artiste himself. As a boy comedian he worked with the Jefferson company, but he soon outgrew it and its programme, which consisted mainly of melodramas. Stan was more interested in revue and solo performances, and he was able to indulge this preference when he joined the group run by comedy producer Fred Wescott, better known as Fred Karno (1866-1941). Charlie Chaplin was already a member of the troupe, and Stan Laurel became his stand-in and the second biggest name on the bill.

In 1910, Fred Karno's Comedians went to America, where their satire on 'A Night in an English Music Hall' was highly successful. Two years later, they did another tour in the United States. Chaplin went to work in the cinema with Mack Sennett, the 'King of Comedy', and this was Stan's chance to become Fred Karno's first-liner. But after Chaplin's departure and many internal problems, part of the group went back to Britain. However Stan, plus two of his fellow-comedians, Edgar Hurley and his wife, decided to stay on in America with their own act. At first they called themselves 'The Three Comiques' and 'Hurley, Stan and Wren', and later they became 'The Keystone Trio'.

When this group eventually separated, Stan joined up with 'Cooke and Hamilton' – Alice and Baldwin (Baldy) Cooke – to form 'The Stan Jefferson Trio'. In 1916 they performed their first sketch, 'The Crazy Cracksman', and it was a success.

In March 1917 the trio was playing in the Hippodrome Theater in Los Angeles. Their director, Adolph Ramish, realized that in Stan Laurel he had a major new comic talent. He watched the act a few times, took a look at how audiences were reacting, and said to Stan, 'It's my personal opinion you're funnier than Chaplin!': this to a young revue artiste who had often had to understudy for Chaplin and had been his 'straight man' whilst working for Fred Karno. The audience never realized it was not the real Chaplin they were watching, and sometimes even his fellow actors were not aware either.

Although Adolph Ramish was the first to see Stan's potential as a film comedian, his name appears far less often in the annals of the cinema than that of Carl Laemmle, of whom more anon. Ramish persuaded former theatre comedian Robbin ('Bobby') Williamson, director at Kalem Studios, to make a short film with Stan as an idiotic character who wore normal clothes but a Napoleonic three-cornered

Lucky Dog, (1917): Laurel and Hardy's first film together, though they appeared separately rather than as a duo.

hat on his head. The film, *Nuts in May,* was what we would now call a 'pilot', made in the hope that Ramish would be able to attract a distributor's attention to the talents of Stan Jefferson. It was shown in the Hippodrome in front of an audience which included the director of Universal, the diminutive German-born Carl Laemmle. It also included Stan's former colleague, Charles Chaplin, who had come from Britain, made himself a very good living as a film comedian and was now planning to start making his own films. As he watched *Nuts in May,* Chaplin must have realized that he was looking at an artist of the same calibre as himself, and from the same background, who was about to establish a niche in America just as strong as his own. After the preview of *Nuts in May* (there are no copies of it left in existence), he and Stan went out for a meal. Chaplin suggested the two of them work together, and Stan jumped at the idea. Chaplin had gained a great deal of experience in the cinema, and times were hard for revue artistes like Stan.

Carl Laemmle also liked *Nuts in May* very much, and offered Stan a one-year contract. Stan hesitated at first, in the knowledge that his former colleague wanted them to work together. He contacted Chaplin to find out what his plans were, but one of the phrases Charlie had learned in America was 'Don't call me, I'll call you!' Stan Jefferson waited all his life for Chaplin to call, but it never happened.

The 'Hickory Hiram' two-reelers Stan made at Universal Studios were not funny. The distributors had trouble selling them, and Stan's contract with Laemmle was not renewed. Stan ended up back on the stage, with the Australian Mae Charlotte Dahlberg, who had also appeared in the 'Hickory Hiram' films. Together they formed a new vaudeville act: Stan and Mae Laurel.

Whenever Stan was asked where the name Laurel came from, he would always say he could not remember. The well-known story that

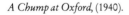

A Chump at Oxford, (1940).

The Second Hundred Years, (1927), with Stanley 'Tiny' Sandford as the warder in a carefully posed still.

he gave up the name Stan Jefferson because there were thirteen letters in it comes from Mae Laurel. Stan couldn't remember where the new name came from, but Mae could. In 1953 she told John McCabe, Laurel and Hardy's friend and biographer, how he had been worrying about those thirteen letters for a long while, until in a dressing-room he saw a picture of a classical Roman general wearing a traditional laurel garland. Somehow the name fitted, and it became the name he used in his films, though it was not until 1934 that he had it changed by deed poll.

In 1917 Stan Laurel caught the attention of Gilbert M. 'Broncho Billy' Anderson, the predecessor of William S. Hart as the great screen cowboy, and co-founder of the Essanay Company in Chicago, which turned out large numbers of one-reel Westerns. Essanay came from 'S and A' – the first letters of the surnames of its founders, Anderson and George K. Spoor. Broncho Billy had come to California from Chicago to make comedies under the label of Sunkist or Sun Lite. At the time, Stan Laurel was making a two-reeler, *Lucky Dog,* for Anderson. In the film, Stan is held up by a fat street-thief with a large moustache: 'Put 'em both up, insect, before I comb your hair with lead!' says the title. His adversary, brandishing a Colt .45, is none other than Oliver Norvell Hardy.

Anderson produced a number of films with Stan Laurel, including parodies of popular feature films such as *Blood and Sand* with Rudolph Valentino (this came out as *Mud and Sand,* with Stan playing Rhubarb Vaselino), and *Robin Hood* with Douglas Fairbanks, which became *Rob 'Em Good.* The latter name had already been used for a Bull Montana film, however, so it was changed to *When Knights Were Cold.*

Although Anderson's comedies with Stan Laurel were moderately successful, the partnership did not last. Stan went back to vaudeville, and in between appearances made a dozen one- and two-reelers for the young producer Hal E. Roach. These are discussed in a later chapter of this book.

In 1924, Stan worked for producer Joe Rock (1891-1984). Together they made a number of shorts and more parodies on famous films of the time. These included *Monsieur Don't Care* (from Valentino's *Monsieur Beaucare*), *Snow Hawk*, *West of Hot Dog* (a parody of the cowboy hit *West Of Pecos*), *Half a Man* and *Dr Pyckle and Mr Pryde*. Joe Rock would hire studios from Universal and use the sets from other films which had been finished. In the few days between the last day of filming and the demolition of the set, Stan Laurel and Joe Rock's technicians would move into the studio to make their two-reelers. So, for example, *Dr Pyckle and Mr Pryde* was filmed on sets from the Lon Chaney classic, *The Hunchback of Notre Dame*. Joe Rock called his films Stan Laurel Comedies.

The two-reelers from 1924 still occasionally appear on television and in special showings by film museums and independent cinemas. But the public tends to be more used to Laurel and Hardy films and the solo performances by Laurel are not greatly appreciated these days.

Stan Laurel's contract with Joe Rock was for twelve months. By September 1924, three months before the contract expired, they had already made the planned number of films. So Stan went on to work with Hal Roach as a scriptwriter and 'ideas man'. Here he got to know many of the great stars of cinema comedy including Ben Turpin, Charley Chase, Edgar Kennedy, James Finlayson, Billy Gilbert, Billy Bevan, Snub Pollard and the 'Our Gang' team. He also bumped into the generously proportioned actor with whom he had appeared seven years earlier in *Lucky Dog*: Oliver Hardy. Roach called his collection of acting

The Laurel and Hardy Murder Case, (1930).

talent 'The Comedy All-Stars'. Stan worked as a director for Roach as well as writing scripts and producing ideas, but Roach did not let him act. This ex-lorry-driver took great care to ensure that his films were of the highest technical quality, and we have him to thank for the fact that there are still good copies of his films around today. Stan's red hair and light blue eyes showed up bleached on the orthochromatic film used between about 1917 and 1925 and he had to use a great deal of make-up. It was not until people started using panchromatic film, whose emulsion is sensitive to the whole spectrum of colour, that his eyes, and thus his facial expressions, could at last be shown to advantage on the cinema screen. This is why the films he made before 1926 are of very poor quality and almost unshowable. In addition, many of these early two- and three-reelers have been lost because they were made on unstable nitrate film. This also applies to most of his later shorts and feature films, but fortunately they have been transferred to fireproof acetate film.

On the advice of the head of his production department, F. Richard (Dicky) Jones, Roach allowed Stan Laurel to play in *Get 'Em Young* in place of Oliver Hardy, who was off work because of a burn on his arm he had incurred whilst cooking a meal. Then Jones asked Laurel to write himself a part in the film he was currently scripting, *Slipping Wives* (1927). *Slipping Wives* is an inconsequential little film about an artist, his beautiful wife, a clumsy butler and a lover in the person of a travelling paint salesman. The butler is Oliver Hardy, minus moustache and with his hair slicked down with pomade. Stan Laurel is the lover, a simple businessman in a conventional suit and bow tie. Very much stock comedy characters, in fact, but whilst the other actors dutifully play out their roles ('we're making another film tomorrow') there is a certain magic to the scenes where Stan and Oliver are acting together: it is obvious that there is some sort of future for them together as a comedy

That's My Wife, (1929): 'Either he goes, or I go!' says Mrs Hardy (Vivien Oakland), pointing to Stan.

team. Stan Laurel's first appearance follows the title (written by Stan?): 'Out of nowhere, going nowhere, delivering paint.' Even in this early film, the Laurel and Hardy spirit is present. Although the parts were not written for them as a duo, they go together like ham and eggs.

On the front of 3 Argyle Street on the edge of Ulverston in Lancashire, there is a plaque reading:

STAN LAUREL
WAS BORN
IN THIS HOUSE
16TH JUNE 1890

Also in Ulverston, at 4c Upper Brook Street, is the Laurel and Hardy Museum. This cramped little building, formerly a barn, is packed full of photographs, posters and newspaper articles about Laurel and Hardy. The museum is a hobby for the former mayor of the town, Bill Cubin.

In August 1984, the 5th International Congress of 'Sons of the Desert', the Laurel and Hardy fan club, took place in Ulverston, and the delegates received a hospitable welcome from the whitewashed café which was named 'Stan Laurel' in 1976.

4

Oliver Hardy

The urn containing the ashes of Oliver Hardy is in the Valhalla Memorial Park Cemetery at 10621 Victoria Boulevard in Hollywood. On it is inscribed:

OLIVER HARDY
(1892–1957)
A GENIUS OF COMEDY

His talent brought joy and
laughter to all the world.

The inscription was placed there in 1977, twenty years after his death, by the international Laurel and Hardy fan club, Sons of the Desert.

In literature about Laurel and Hardy, the person of Stan Laurel tends to be more emphasized and described in greater depth than that of Oliver Hardy. In the two authorized biographies of Laurel mentioned earlier, and in books and articles on the two of them it is primarily Stan who appears as the creative mind behind their success, the all-round British comic with the great comic intellect. Oliver Hardy tends to be regarded as the 'feeder', or Stan's fall-guy, and it has been said that if Oliver Hardy had not met Stan Laurel he would soon have had to give up acting. It was only in combination with Stan Laurel that Oliver Hardy could develop his full potential and reach the level of success that he did. Whether or not this is true is still open to question.

Oliver Hardy was a very subtle pantomime actor, a man who despite his girth could still act with grace and even a certain amount of elegance. His face has nothing particularly funny about it *per se*, nor is it particularly expressive. But he had the ability to put his feelings across to the audience without the use of words, for example when getting angry with Stan's stupidity or when he feels he has been sold short by somebody. One of Oliver Hardy's most famous trademarks is the exasperated glare at the camera, suddenly involving the audience directly. This communication between screen and audience was new, and Oliver Hardy made no comment when people such as Bob Hope and Groucho Marx started following his example. These asides, where the actor in effect steps out of the situation he is in, were a technique long used in the theatre, and writers such as Shakespeare and Molière unleashed whole long monologues on their audiences. With his soulful gaze into the camera, Oliver invites the audience to share his exasperation with the situation he is in and arouses a feeling of being somehow superior to the people and events in the film, a kind of pleasurable shudder at one's good fortune at not being involved in the action. Like many good comics, both Oliver Hardy and Stan Laurel made light of their use of this technique, preferring to shrug it off and say, as they did on occasions, that they did their best to make people laugh and that was all.

We can see in films like *Big Business* and *Two Tars* that Stan and Oliver have the powerful ability to appear unmoved, even stoical about the misfortunes that beset them, as though they are more interested in what happens next than the fact that they are victims of the whims of fate. Neither of them ever explained why this had such a powerfully humorous effect as far as the audience was concerned.

The endless fumbling with his bow-tie, twisting it back and forth like a child with a new piece of cloth he doesn't particularly like, his habit of tapping the tips of his fat fingers together to show impatience, the use of his full name (Oliver *Norvell* Hardy) when he wanted to make an impression; the affectionate way he introduces his partner (I'd like you to meet my friend, Mr Laurel'), and the arrogant way in which he will

Thundering Fleas, (1926): Oliver Hardy.

push Stan aside ('Let *me* do that'), his graceful dancing (see *The Music Box* or *Way Out West),* his calm statement: 'Well, here's another nice mess you've gotten me into' (not 'another *fine* mess', as he is frequently misquoted as saying, probably from the title of their 1930 short, *Another Fine Mess):* Oliver Hardy had a clearly defined set of traits which went to make his screen personality. For wit, the two are each other's equals, and together, in their best films, their acting is nothing short of genius.

Norvell Hardy (the name Oliver appeared later on) was born on 18 January 1892 in Harlem, Georgia. He was the son of lawyer Oliver Hardy and his wife, Emily Norvell. At birth, he weighed 14lb, the

The Bohemian Girl, (1936): Oliver Hardy and Darla Hood.

weight of a healthy one-year-old. When Norvell was eighteen months old, his father died, and Emily had five children to look after on her own (Norvell had two older stepbrothers and two stepsisters from his mother's first marriage). The family all loved singing and young Norvell joined in with gusto. Then Emily Hardy went to manage the Baldwin Hotel in Milledgeville, Georgia, and every day after school Norvell could be found in the entrance hall, watching the guests in fascination. This 'lobby-watching' remained a lifelong pastime, and his career as an actor was in no small part due to his ability to portray different types of human being. Norvell Hardy particularly enjoyed watching the theatre folk that stayed in the Baldwin Hotel on a regular basis, and he listened

Early to Bed, (1928): Top: At the beginning of the film, Laurel and Hardy have only a park bench to their name, but Oliver inherits his uncle's fortune. He takes on Stan as his butler.
Bottom: Stan wants to leave his job and does everything he can to be dismissed.

eagerly to all their enthralling stories. When he was eight, he ran away from home to join Coburn's Minstrels as a singer. The leader of the group, Charles Coburn (not to be confused with *the* Charles Coburn) was a friend of Emily Hardy's, so the young musical adventurer had a careful eye kept on him during the beginning of his career.

In 1906, Hardy was singing in a cinema in Atlanta for 50¢ a day, leading sessions of community singing which were common at film performances in the southern United States. In 1910, he opened his own small cinema in Milledgeville, financed partly by his mother. At eighteen, he was the youngest cinema manager in the whole of the country. As well as running the cinema, he also operated the projector and sang too, by popular request. His one great aim in life was to become a vocalist, and his idol was Enrico Caruso.

The one- and two-reelers he showed in his cinema at weekends (it was closed on weekdays) gave him the idea of going into films. He was not impressed by what he saw on the screen, and was convinced he could do better himself. In 1913, Norvell Hardy went to Jacksonville, Florida, to work as an extra with the Lubin Motion Pictures Company for a few dollars a day. He changed his name to Oliver Hardy, after his father, and kept his eyes open. He was a 'Johnny-on-the-spot', always around at the right place and the right time to do what anyone wanted him to; even when he did not need to be in the studios he was still to be found there. He helped cameramen, acted as a script-clerk, assisted directors and ran around with props and scenery. He learned the business in a very short space of time and became very much part of the whole Lubin machine, even belonging to the studio baseball club. Whilst there, he would have his hair cut in the local Italian barber's. The story of Hardy's alternative name, Babe, is this: the Figaro character used to cut the hair of many of the Lubin employees, so they would all be sitting in a row waiting their turn. Whilst cutting Oliver's rotund head of hair, he would trip his way around the chair, constantly murmuring: 'Nice-a-baby, nice-a-baby.' So his fellow-employees christened him Babe, and the name stuck within the film business from 1913 onwards.

Oliver Hardy's figure obviously made him ideally suited to playing 'heavies' in films. As a serious actor with an unshaven face, heavily made-up eyebrows and protruding stomach, he was perfect, and he also played policemen with considerable skill. In 1915, he and comedian Bobby Ray made a two-reeler, *The Paper-Hanger's Helper,* with Hardy as the straight man and Bobby Ray the idiot. Although Ray was fairly small and his appearance was not that far removed from Stan Laurel's, it shows even in this early stage in his career that Oliver Hardy did not really shine as an actor unless he was playing opposite someone else.

In 1917 he went to New York to act with Pathé, Gaumont, Edison and Vitagraph. With Vitagraph, he played in Larry Semon comedies, and appeared in such films as *The Perfect Clown, Kid Speed* and the old version of *The Wizard of Oz.* By the end of 1924 he was working for Hal Roach and had been working as an actor for ten years, appearing in

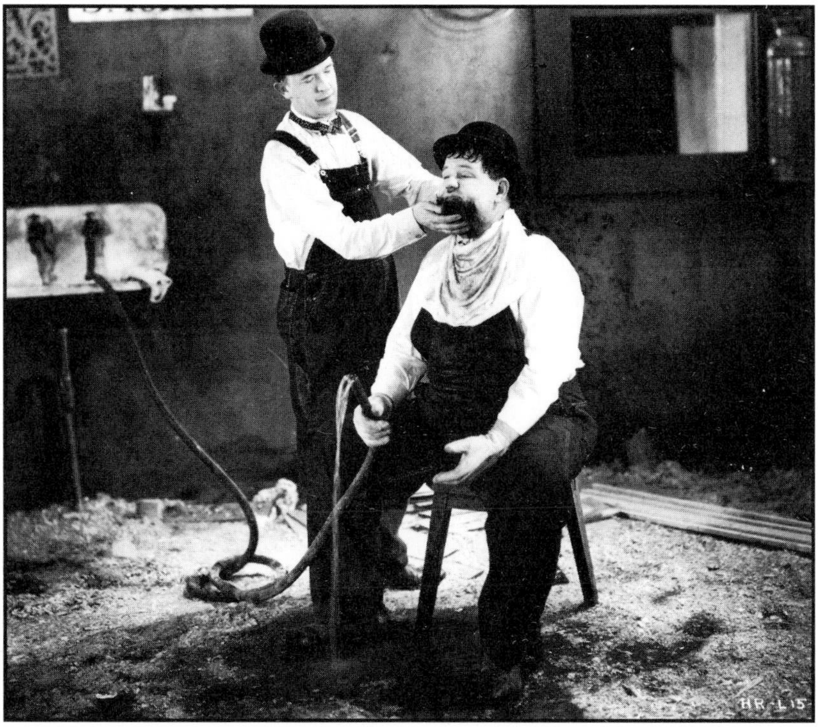

Busy Bodies, (1933).

nearly two hundred films but still not having established himself with any particular renown as an actor. Roach took him on not for his comic appearance but simply as a player of minor roles in films like *Rex, King of the Wild Horses* and Charley Chase comedies like *Fluttering Hearts, Crazy Like a Fox* and *Long Fliv the King*.

Less than a year after he joined Hal Roach, Hardy married actress Myrtle Lee Reeves. He became very much the settled husband, joining the Lakeside Golf Club (where he played with W.C. Fields and Bing Crosby) and becoming addicted to playing cards and horse-racing. Hal Roach was a fellow-devotee of the latter and they often went to the races together. Oliver 'Babe' Hardy was a gregarious type, the prototype fat and jolly man. He got on well with everyone and would often amuse his colleagues on the set or in the dressing-rooms by telling jokes about blacks in an exaggerated southern accent, though he was not a racist by any stretch of the imagination. At the age of eighteen his best friend in Milledgeville was a negro boy named Sam, and for years as a baby and then a toddler he had been brought up by a black housekeeper he called Mama; his mother he called Miss Emily.

In 1926 Oliver Hardy and Stan Laurel were part of the Hal Roach All Stars. Other studios liked stars with catchy names, but Hal Roach thought all his actors and actresses were 'absolute toppers', even Pete the Wonderdog. However, this concealed the fact that he had no particular talent under his roof, and it was chief producer and part-time director Leo McCarey who was the first to combine the abilities of Stan Laurel and Oliver Hardy in the two-reeler *Putting Pants on Philip* (1927), the first true Laurel and Hardy picture. Oliver Hardy was now thirty-five and Stan Laurel thirty-seven.

5

Stan Laurel and Oliver Hardy

Given that they worked for the same studio and both belonged to 'The Hal Roach Comedy All Stars', it was logical that Stan Laurel and Oliver Hardy should start appearing in the same comedies together, though separately rather than as a duo. This they did in thirteen films before Hal Roach and his chief producer Leo McCarey put them together in *Putting Pants on Philip* (1927). This was the first two-reeler produced specifically as a Laurel and Hardy comedy, though it was not distributed as such. Whenever Stan Laurel was asked how the two of them got together, he would always reply that it just happened naturally.

And this rings true, for the names Laurel and Hardy somehow go together, just like Marks and Spencer or Fortnum and Mason. So it was partly because people got used to hearing the two names mentioned together in the same breath, but partly also because they *looked* as though they belonged together.

Although Hal Roach played a major part in putting them together as a team (apart from anything else, he more or less gave them *carte blanche,* which is something we have to thank him for), it was really Leo McCarey who 'discovered' Laurel and Hardy. McCarey directed Bing Crosby in *Going My Way* (1944), and Cary Grant and Irene Dunn in *The Awful Truth* (1937), for which he received two Oscars, as well as the best of the Marx Brothers films, *Duck Soup* (1933). He also made films with W.C. Fields and Harold Lloyd. After a short career as a lawyer, Leo McCarey joined Hal Roach as a gag-writer, director and producer for the 'Our Gang' shorts and Charley Chase comedies.

One of the most important things McCarey did when putting together the Laurel and Hardy films was to drastically slow down the frenetic pace of most comedy up until that time. He removed the

Leo McCarey (1898-1969), the producer/director/scriptwriter at Hal Roach Studios who 'discovered' Laurel and Hardy.

influence of Mack Sennett from the films he made for Hal Roach. When Peter Bogdanovich interviewed him for the Oral History department of the American Film Institute a few months before his death, McCarey said: 'We're all working too fast. We've got to get away from these jerky movements and work out at a normal speed.' At the time, this was a daring move to make.

So there were to be no more high-speed chase sequences, no people wearing odd clothes. To make them look more serious and normal, the two were given the famous derby hats and high-collared coats. They were sometimes accused of having borrowed the trademark of the derby from Chaplin. At the beginning of the century, it was common for market traders in the poorer districts of London to wear these hats and coats to give the impression of being reliable, upright traders. British music-hall artistes and American vaudeville players spotted this and took over the workaday costume, just as Chaplin had done. Admittedly it was Chaplin who was the first to do so, but this was not simply a case of plagiarism.

Laurel and Hardy always play 'ordinary' people: painters, carpenters, boot-blacks, detectives, butlers, legionnaires, sailors. Their neat clothing and self-conscious presence shows their desire first and foremost to be taken seriously. So the two men we see walking onto the screen are not idiots or clowns, but people trying to be good, respectable members of society. The fact that they never manage to do so is not their fault. In the years of economic crisis, they had the audience identifying with them from the word go. They were the underdogs: everything works against them, and they rarely manage anything approaching normal relations with the opposite sex. The only exceptions to the latter are in *Scram!* (1932) and *Them Thar Hills* (1942) where they have a close female friend in the persons of Vivien Oakland and Mae Busch, respectively. But on the whole, the often very attractive women who play their wives spend their time throwing things at them, get in their way and constantly remind them of their pathetic position in society. In the 1930s there must have been countless men who had reached the end of their tethers and saw something of themselves in Laurel and Hardy. When, in *Thicker than Water* (1935), Mrs Hardy (Daphne Pollard) sits eating her breakfast and wearing a striped summer dress with a ribbon in her hair, and Oliver Hardy reaches out to caress her face with his fingertips, she bites his hand without even looking up from her plate. So it is hardly surprising that with a few exceptions women do not have a very high status in Laurel and Hardy films. They are portrayed as weak, spiteful and full of sick humour. Laurel and Hardy are not popular with the feminists , and they have been accused of displaying a latent homosexual relationship. The pair quite happily share the same bed in their worn-out pyjamas, and the slightly tasteless scene in *Berth Marks* (1929) where they share a sleeping compartment speaks for itself. Be we see these sexual overtones again in *Laughing*

The Live Ghost, (1934).

Gravy (1931), *Leave 'Em laughing* (1928), *They Go Boom* (1929, floating on a Restwell Air Mattress), *The Fixer Uppers* (1935) and *A Chump at Oxford* (1940). In *Their First Mistake* (1932), Oliver Hardy has been hit with a broom and thrown out of the door by his wife, Mae Busch. Stan lies on the bed with his clothes on, and Oliver sits on the edge.

Stan: What did she say?
Oliver: You heard what she said!
Stan: Well, what's the matter with her, anyway?
Oliver: Oh, I don't know. She always says that I think more of you than I do of her.
Stan: Well, you do, don't you?
Oliver: We won't go into that!

In *The Music Box,* a three-reeler made in 1932 which received an Oscar as the Best Short Subject of the year, the irate nanny hits piano-transporter Oliver Hardy over the head with a baby's bottle. Stan feels Oliver's head, inspects the bump coming up, and promptly kicks the woman in the behind. Imagine that happening in today's cinema! The woman pushes her pram along to a policeman, points to Oliver Hardy and says: 'He kicked me, right in the middle of my daily duties!' Nor did lines like 'Mr Hardy was married – Mr Laurel was also unhappy' go down very well with women.

We may or may not agree with Molly Haskell, who writes:

> With their disaster-prone bodies and their exclusive relationship that not only shuts out women but questions their very necessity, they constitute a two-man wrecking team of female – that is, civilized and bourgeois – society...The male duo, from Laurel and Hardy to Abbott and Costello, is almost by definition, or by metaphor, latently homosexual; a union of opposites (tall/short, thin/fat, straight/comic) who, like husband and wife, combine to make a whole.

If Laurel and Hardy represent the acme of film comedy, then Hiram 'Beanie' Walker's linking titles are also masterpieces of their kind. He was responsible for the titles from 1926 *(45 Minutes From Hollywood)* to 1932 *(Pack Up Your Troubles),* and all of them are brilliant pieces of prose which have lost nothing of their evocative power and wry humour. It is an unfortunate fact that, although much of the humour of the films has a universal appeal, the titles do no translate well and in foreign-language versions of the films they are a shadow of their original selves.

'Beanie' Walker's writing talents extended to scripts as well. Some of the finest examples can be heard on two LPs produced by United

Artists in their series, 'The Golden Age of Comedy', the first entitled 'Laurel and Hardy' and the second 'Another Fine Mess'. The fourth track on side 1 of the first record is an extract from *Thicker than Water* (1935), and is called 'Furniture Payment'. The scene involves Stan Laurel, Oliver Hardy, James Finlayson (who has come to see the Hardy family to collect some money for some furniture bought on hire-purchase) and Daphne Pollard as Mrs Hardy. Mrs Hardy has given the money to Oliver, and asks why Finlayson has not received it.

Mrs Hardy: Oliver: Did I or did I not give you the money to pay on the furniture?
Oliver: You certainly did...
Mrs Hardy: Then why wasn't it paid?
Oliver: Why, I give it to him to pay it *for* me.
Mrs Hardy: Then, what did *you* do with it?
Stan: I gave it back to him.
Oliver: You gave it to *me?*
Stan: Yeah, I gave it to you to pay my room and board. Then you gave it to her, *remember?*
Mrs Hardy: Do you mean to say that the money that *he* gave to *you,* that *you* gave to *him,* that *he* gave to *me,* was the same money that *I* gave to *him* to pay him?
Stan: Well, if it was the money that *you* gave to *him* to give to me to pay to *him,* it must have been the money *I* gave *him* to give to *you* to pay my rent, didn't I?
Mrs Hardy: Mr Finlayson, I owe you an apology!
Finlayson: ...and thirty-seven dollars!
Mrs Hardy: Then this money must belong to you.
Finlayson: And the next time I want my payment without any detour. She gave it to *you* and you gave it to *him* and who gave it to *what!* You're all nuts!
Mrs Hardy: You big dumb-bell, I can't trust you to do a thing – and as for *you,* I've a good mind of throwing you out!
Stan: You can't do it.
Mrs Hardy: I can't do it?
Stan: No, 'cause I paid my room and board in advance, and I gave it to *him!*
Oliver: What do you mean, you gave it to *me?* That was the money that *she* gave to *me* and I gave to *you* to give to *him.* Then *you* gave it back to *me* and I had to give it to *her* to give to *him!*
Stan: Was that the money that *she* gave to *him* that I gave to *you* to give...
Oliver: Why, certainly!
Stan: Well, if she wants to give it to *him,* that's *her* business, no use you and I arguing about it!

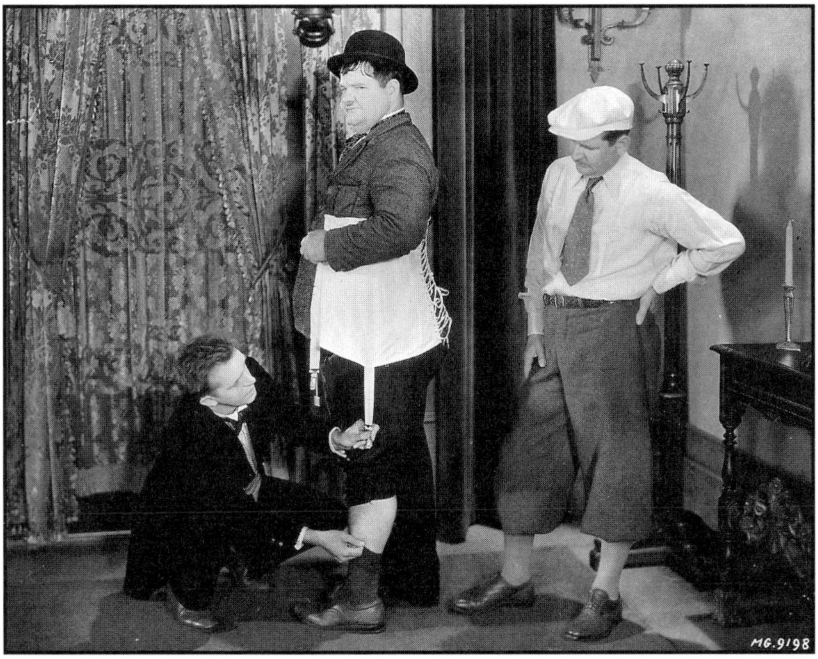

Twice Two, (1933).

Laurel and Hardy's small talk is also an attraction in itself. In *Going Bye-Bye!* (1934), Oliver Hardy says to a woman on the telephone: 'Excuse me please, my ear is full of milk!' It looks odd on paper, but it fits in with the events on screen. Hardy has put a newly opened milk bottle to his ear. In *Pardon Us* (1931), Laurel and Hardy are receiving lessons in a prison classroom full of unsavoury types. The whole atmosphere is reminiscent of *Metropolis,* full of depressing grimness. 'Fin' greets his pupils: 'Good Morning, dear playmates!'

Fin: Now then, what is a blizzard?
Stan: A blizzard is the outside of a buzzard.
Fin: Three goes into nine how many times?
Stan: Three times...
Fin: Correct!
Stan: ...and two left over.
Fin: What are you laughing at?
Oliver: There's only one left over!
Fin: All right now. Spell 'needle'.
Oliver: N-e-i-d-l-e.
Fin: There's no *i* in needle.
Stan: Then it's a rotten needle!

Talking of James Finlayson: all true Laurel and Hardy fans have a soft spot for the small Scotsman. James (or Jimmy) Finlayson's gimmick is shooting his left eyebrow upwards whilst simultaneously screwing up his right eye to a narrow slit. The effect is particularly vicious-looking. Fin tends to display this habit when he hears something he is unable to

Men O'War, (1928): Top: Laurel and Hardy trying to buy a round of drinks with only 15¢ to their name. Bottom: The preliminaries to a mini-naval battle on a boating lake.

understand. The event has no immediate effect on him, for it takes some long while for his brain to process it, and then he reacts: first the abrupt arm and leg movements of someone suffering from motor disturbance, and then a close-up of the extraordinary eyebrow-raising trick.

Like his friend and colleague, Stan Laurel, Finlayson began by travelling around Britian with a variety company. He then went to America in 1916 as a balding actor with a pronounced moustache and appeared in Mack Sennett comedies. In 1923 he found himself working for Hal Roach, and played beside Stan Laurel in *A Man About Town* (1923) and *Smithy* (1924).

In 1929 he found his feet as a comedian playing the irate citizen who refuses to buy a Christmas tree in the Laurel and Hardy film, *Big Business*. He went on to appear in thirty-three Laurel and Hardy films. He was the barkeeper and boat-rental man in *Men O'War*, Colonel Buckshot in *Another Fine Mess*, Oliver's impatient father-in-law in *Me and My Pal*, the general in *Pack up Your Troubles* and the unforgettable greedy saloon-owner in *Way Out West*. At the end of the latter film we hear him crying, after a noisy indoor chase, 'You...son of a bitch!'

Was this a piece of ad-libbing by Finlayson? It is possible, for it seems unlikely that the script should have included this earthy piece of American English. Since it is hard to hear it amongst the clamour of the room, it must have slipped through the censor's net. Certainly, it is the kind of thing one might very easily say in the face of such circumstances: for once, Finlayson is not acting, he is being his real self.

When the sound film, *The Jazz Singer*, received its world première on 6 October 1927, and was far better received than any of the sound films that had been shown so far, Hal Roach decided to go into sound full-time. Initially he continued making silent shorts as well, and later, as the clumsy sound on disc system (where the soundtrack was created using gramophone records) was replaced by optical recordings on the surface of the film itself, he made the transition to sound. For some actors, the invention of the sound film was a disaster: they had the acting ability, but their voices simply were not suited to film-making. But Laurel and Hardy were all-round artists, and they used the new medium to the full. Audiences liked the combination of Oliver Hardy's Georgia accent and Stan Laurel's Lancashire/Cockney/Hollywood hybrid of a voice. One problem was the fact that films now had less international appeal, since the dialogue was in English, and Hal Roach was going to lose a sizeable part of the market for his comedies as a result. But they were not going to be put off that easily, so they made somewhat primitive French, Spanish, German and Italian versions of their films as well. Thus each film had to be made five times, using actors who generally spoke the languages concerned perfectly. Laurel and Hardy simply had their scripts printed phonetically on big boards and read them out as best they could. There are still 35mm copies of these foreign-language Laurel and Hardy comedies in Europe, and we have the interesting spectacle of Laurel and Hardy speaking their lines without knowing what they are saying.

Hal Roach was very fortunate in having Metro-Goldwyn-Mayer as his distributor, for they made sure his shorts and the best of his feature films reached audiences in cinemas the world over. The publicity department of MGM did a good job with the Laurel and Hardy films, and although they were often used to support a main feature, they were still held in very high regard by the cinema-going public. Not infrequently the mere mention of there being a Laurel and Hardy film on the programme would get audiences to come along to watch a feature they would not otherwise have gone to see.

Countless stills were made from the films, to be displayed outside cinemas and reprinted in newspaper and magazine articles. MGM even supplied small photographs to manufacturers of wallets, to be placed inside the transparent plastic pocket so that people would find themselves carrying a picture of one of MGM's stars around with them wherever they went. But none of these stills actually showed real scenes from the film. They would be taken after the actual sequence or the whole film had been shot, with the actors resuming roughly the same position as in the film. Stan Laurel often directed these still-photography sessions himself, knowing from his vaudeville days how important it was from an advertising point of view to have pictures of your artists in the lobby of the theatre. Every actor or actress did his or her best to look as funny as possible in the stills, so inevitably they are not an accurate reflection of the scene they are supposed to portray. Some of these stills have quite a story to tell, and all of them are lively and full of interest for the Laurel and Hardy fan, giving as much pleasure as watching the film itself. Some of the photographers who worked for other studios were credited for their work, and if they are still alive they can have the pleasure of seeing their pictures reproduced in books about the films, but the stills photographers used by Hal Roach were, and still are, anonymous. However, their work is very much in demand in Britain and America, and an original numbered series in mint condition can fetch $1000, whilst an individual photo from one of the older two-reelers will reach more than a $100 if it is in good condition. *Collecting Movie Memorabilia* (first published in 1977 by the Arco Corporation in New York) and *The Movie Collector's Catalog* (published by the Cumming Publishing Corporation in New Rochelle) are two good places to find an indication of how much a still photograph may be worth.

The noble art of cinematic pie-throwing is supposed to have been begun by Mabel Normand throwing one at Ben Turpin. Puddings had been thrown on a regular basis on the English stage as early as the eighteenth century, and later in 1897 they were a frequent feature of performances in Britain by Fred Karno's theatre company. As far as we know, the first pie ever to be used for comic effect in the United States was in *The Corn Cures* which was premièred on 17 March 1898 in the Weber and Fields Music Hall in New York. Mack Sennett comedies regularly included pie-throwing scenes, and other film-makers did not exactly shy away from this particular method of raising a laugh. But it reaches its apotheosis in the Laurel and Hardy film *The Battle of the Century* (1927), directed by Clyde Bruckman, Hal Roach and Leo McCarey. The climax of this silent two-reeler is a huge pie-fight in the middle of the street. Hal Roach wanted to make sure his audiences saw hundreds of pies being thrown and Stan Laurel himself said; 'Look, if we make a pie picture, let's make a pie picture to end all pie pictures. Let's give them so many pies there will never be room for any more pie pictures in the whole history of the movies!'

But he was wrong, even though this greatest pie-throwing sequence in the history of film used up an entire day's production of real pies (mostly fruit) from the Los Angeles Pie Company. Estimates of the number actually thrown have increased with the passing of the years and now stand at several thousand.

The Battle of the Century is one of the funniest, possibly the funniest two-reeler ever made. The fight begins when delivery-man Charlie Hall slips on a banana skin with his tray of pies. Henry Miller took it

Two scenes from *The Bohemian Girl,* (1936): With Laurel and Hardy and the dog, Laughing Gravy.

seriously enough to write an essay about it in *The Golden Age* in 1945, and four years later James Agee wrote a much-quoted article on the subject for *Life* magazine.

The scene has erotic undertones, too, with Anita Garvin and her stunning dress falling backwards onto a pie outside the Taft Building and delicately wiping her behind as she stands up again. A patient in a dentist's chair, mouth wide open, get a mouthful of pie instead of a whirring drill; newly cleaned shoes lose their shine in a lake of fresh cream. The scene is a veritable orgy of flying pies, not a little decadent in the poverty-stricken America of 1927.

Eight years later, in 1935, Ralph Staub attempted the same thing for Jack Warner in his short film, *Keystone Hotel*, in which a lengthy pie fight takes place during a fashion show. In come the Keystone Cops; Ford Sterling cries, 'Stop, in the name of the law!' and is hit full in the face by a pie. Director Staub was attempting to revive the genre of slapstick comedy in the cinema and took on a number of comedians for the purpose, including Ben Turpin, Chester Conklin, Jack Duffy and Dewey Robinson. At the end of the two-reel *Keystone Hotel* even the camera lens falls victim to the hail of flying pies: the picture is blanked out by one and this is the cue for the closing credits – 'The End, Vitagraph Varieties'.

It is interesting that almost every compilation of old Mack Sennett silent comedies anywhere in the world seems to include the pie-throwing sequence from *Keystone Hotel*. This is despite the fact that it is neither a Sennett film nor a silent comedy, but an imitation, a perfect re-make which is considered today to contain one of the classic pie-throwing scenes of the 1920s.

After the beginning of the series of Laurel and Hardy Comedies, Stan Laurel and Oliver Hardy started using their own names as screen identities: a wise move, since characters who bore a different name to the actors portraying them remained the property of the studios they worked for. This meant that Laurel and Hardy could take the characters round with them to other studios if they wished. This they did at the beginning of the forties, when they made eight feature films for studios other than Hal Roach's: six for 20th Century-Fox and two for MGM. In addition, they made the mediocre French/Italian co-production, *Atoll K*. These features were far less amusing than their previous work, even though a bad Laurel and Hardy is often better than a good film by another comic duo such as Abbott and Costello.

Atoll K appeared in a number of different versions. The original French/Italian version, produced by Raymond Eger for Les Films Sirius and Fortezza Films, lasts ninety-eight minutes. In the United States the film was not shown for three years, but eventually it was distributed under the title *Robinson Crusoeland* or *Utopia*, with a running time of eight-two minutes. In 1954 Exploitation Productions turned it into a half-hour film for television. But, long or short, it was an abysmal film. The original time budgeted for making the film was twelve weeks, but eventually it took from 1 April 1950 to 1 April 1951. When the two

The Battle of the Century, (1927): Charlie Hall's pie-van provides the ammunition for the greatest pie-throwing scene in cinema history.

arrived in Paris to make the film, the story had not even been written, so Stan and two American writers hastily put a script together. The director, Leo Joannon, was inexperienced and slow. To add to their problems, Stan Laurel became ill and had to undergo a prostate operation in Paris. He also discovered he was diabetic, and the pain and discomfort he was experiencing (there was a medical team permanently on the set in case he was taken really ill) is visible in the film. He was eating badly and weighed barely eight stone. Once he arrived back in sunny California, with its added advantage of there being no language problem, he gradually recovered. Laurel and Hardy fans have to reckon with the sad fact that this last contribution to the art of film by two of the world's greatest-ever comedians was a total flop.

Likewise, *The Big Noise,* which they made in 1944, was a bad mistake. Sol Wurtzel's last effort after his thirty-year career with 20th Century-Fox was made during the peak of wartime austerity measures and had to be seen to be avoiding any gratuitous waste of materials or props: the pie-throwing extravaganza of *The Battle of the Century* could never have been made in 1944. Any scenes which involved wastage and had to be left in for the sake of the storyline were filmed in one take, and this shows in the clumsy production of some parts of the film. The plot, prophetically enough, revolves around Stan and Oliver being mistaken for private detectives and being hired to look after a mega-bomb which will win the war for the Allies. Although it has many comic possibilities, few of them are exploited and it is plain the Laurel and Hardy are tiring and the end of their career together is looming close on the horizon. Esther Howard, who plays the overweight widow who has her eye on Oliver, turns in an equally poor performance. Even 20th Century-Fox realized the film was a mistake and hid it away amongst second-rate double bills. The critics had no time for it either. Bosley Crowther, of the *New York Times* said:

> A *groan*...Even the most devoted of patrons of Laurel and Hardy films will probably balk at the comics' latest cut-up, *The Big Noise*...It has about as much humour in it as a six-foot hole in the ground...The boys fumble weakly with business for an hour and a quarter – and that is that. Once, long ago, it was funny to see them joust with wet paint and falling beds. But now it is dull and pathetic. And they don't even seem to care.

The fact was that the career of Laurel and Hardy had run out of steam, and it ended not with a bang, but a whimper.

They had been given vitually unlimited artistic freedom by Hal Roach, and Stan Laurel in particular was able to involve himself, albeit unobtrusively, in every aspect of film-making, from editing and camera work to lighting and gag-writing. This was totally out of the question at Fox and MGM, where the rule was play your part and then go home. Nor were their films made in any kind of chronological order as they had been with Hal Roach. Stan Laurel hated this illogical way of making films, imposed on the studios for reasons of economy. What was more, little attention was paid to the advice he and Oliver gave, based on long years of experience.

The director of *Jitterbugs* (1943), *The Big Noise* (1944) and *The Bullfighters* (1945) was Malcolm St Clair, a slapstick expert from the school of Mack Sennett and director of large numbers of 'sophisticated comedies'. When making *Great Guns* (1941), Fox hired the former comedian and long-time acquaintance of Laurel and Hardy, Montague (Monty) Banks to star with them. But it was not totally fair to put their declining fortunes down to the men who directed them and the huge, bureaucratic studios they were working for. It was also true to say that when they left Hal Roach, Laurel and Hardy had passed the peak of their career. They were tired, overworked and no longer as interested in the finished product as they used to be, and they were starting to feel their age, especially Stan Laurel with his youthful screen image. For some clowns, youth and agility are essential qualities. The same happened with comedians such as Harry Langdon and Buster Keaton, both of whom found their physical decline affecting their presence as actors. Stan Laurel was starting to develop wrinkles and turn into a caricature of himself; also he was gaining weight and Oliver was getting thinner, so the physical contrast between the pair was starting to lose its comic effect.

The Big Noise, (1944).

Everyone seems to have realized this, either consciously or unconsciously. In the compilations and TV reviews of their work, it is always the older shorts and the feature films they made before 1941 which tend to be shown. There is simply no comparison between Laurel and Hardy's postwar films and those made between the late 1920s and 1940.

Atoll K, (1950-51): A French/Italian co-production released in the United States as *Robinson Crusoe Land.* Their last and probably worst film.

In December 1954, NBC set Lucille Hardy and Laurel and Hardy's friend and manager Ben Shipman to work on a *This is Your Life* programme about the pair. What could have been a legendary television programme turned into a fiasco. Stan Laurel and Oliver Hardy were lured to the Knickerbocker Hotel in Hollywood by the British impresario, Bernard Delfont, who was visiting America at the time. The programme's presenter, fast-talking Ralph Edwards, confronted them with the terrifying reality in Delfont's hotel room: this was their life. The programme, sponsored by Hazel Bishop Cosmetics, of all people, was shown live, so there was no going back. Oliver Hardy gave confused answers to the questions fired at him, and Stan Laurel said virtually nothing. Later, he said that a few minutes into the programme he was already wishing he had never started: he was a perfectionist, and wished he had been given time to get ready for the broadcast. What was more, ever since he was fourteen it had been against his principles to

Pack Up Your troubles, (1932): Their third feature film.

appear free, especially for a television company, so the reasons for the failure of the programme were not simply artistic and technical. The programme is preserved on video, available from Video Yesteryear, Box C, Sandy Hook, Connecticut, USA. The soundtrack of the recording is also available on LP (Radiola, MR 1104) under the title 'Laurel and Hardy on the Air', also from Video Yesteryear. After this sorry event, Laurel and Hardy both received a 16mm film projector and a film recording their television début.

In some ways, a better reward than this was the fact that Hal Roach Jr promised after the programme that Laurel and Hardy would be making a comeback. At least, that was how they saw it. Roach Jr, who had taken over the running of the studio from his father, offered the two 'old-time' comedians a contract to make four colour films, to be shown by the NBC network in the winter season of 1957-8. If the programmes were a success, they would start on a series.

The new series was to be called 'Laurel and Hardy's Fabulous Fables'. Stan went through his drafts and notes to find sketches and gags that he had never worked through properly and which would be suitable for the new series. Soon there was enough material for eleven one-hour shows. The ingredients of these programmes, English music-hall jokes, plus singing and dancing, were such that with hindsight it was a great stroke of fortune that the programmes never went ahead.

Stan Laurel must have seen the failure of the TV idea coming, whether consciously or not. Despite the enthusiasm he expressed for the new opportunity that had been held out to them, he never put a great deal of effort into the TV series. Also, the fact that Oliver Hardy's health was declining made Stan even less motivated, and neither of them would have been able to get on with TV producers and directors. More than once, Stan said he could not understand either the people that worked in television or the programmes they made: he had no real interest in the new medium at all.

Oliver Hardy died on 7 August 1957. Despite his unfortunate experience with television, Stan Laurel eagerly switched on whenever a film with himself and 'Babe' was shown. He would laugh infectiously at Oliver Hardy and would call the Stan Laurel he saw on screen 'the little fellow', as though it was someone else, and not himself, acting the part. His colleagues in the film business, and his fans, visited him often in the flat Jerry Lewis and Dick Van Dyke rented for him on Oceana Avenue in Santa Monica.

Stan Laurel and his wife Ida were not particularly well off and led a quiet, simple existence. Stan retained his sense of humour until the end of his days. When a group from their fan club, Sons of the Desert, came to present him with a colour television on his birthday, he said, surprised and pleased, 'That's great, that's great. By the way, didn't you know I'm colour-blind?' There must have been a great deal of consternation following this remark, for Laurel and Hardy fans sometimes have a habit of claiming to know more about their idols than the idols themselves.

On 23 February 1965, at the age of seventy-four, Stan Laurel died following a heart attack. The memorial service was held in the Church of the Hills in Hollywood. Dick Van Dyke read a prayer he said he had sent Stan Laurel a few Christmases ago, 'A Prayer for Clowns'.

God bless all clowns
Who star the world with laughter,
Who ring the rafters
With a flying jest,
Who make the world spin merry on its way
And somehow add more beauty to each day.
God bless all clowns
So poor the world would be
Lacking their piquant touch, hilarity,
The belly-laughs, the ringing, lovely mirth
That makes a friendly place of this earth.
God bless all clowns –
Give them a long, good life,
Make bright their way – they're a race apart!
All comest most who turn their hearts' pain
Into a dazzling jest to lift the heart.
God bless all clowns.

Dick Van Dyke told the congregation: 'I'd just like to say to Stan what he always said to all of us when he took his leave: God Bless'. His ashes were placed in the Court of Liberty in the Hollywood Hills Forest Lawn Cemetery. The plaque on it reads:

STAN LAUREL
(1890-1965)
A Master of Comedy
His genius in the art of
humor brought gladness
to the world he loved

Saps at Sea, (1940): The last film Laurel and Hardy made for Hal Roach, and not their best.

HAL ROACH
COMEDY
CAPITOL of the WORLD
Again BRINGS YOU THE
SCREEN'S GREATEST
LAUGHS
Released through United Artists

6

Hal E. Roach

Hal Eugene Roach, born on 14 January 1892 in Elmira, New York State, received an honorary Oscar in 1984 from the Academy of Motion Picture Arts and Sciences for his services to the film industry. He was ninety-two, and this was not his first award from the Academy. He had already received an Oscar in the category Best Short Subject in 1937 for his film, *Based on Education*. His career had begun around 1910, when he worked as a 'stock cowboy' at Universal Studios for $25 a week. Before, he had worked in a number of different jobs in various places, including Alaska.

At Universal, Roach met the then unknown Harold Lloyd, who shared his love of boxing and was working as one of the army of anonymous actors at the studio. The two of them combined their intellectual and financial resources to start a film production company, but this folded after only a few months. Hal Roach went off to Essanay to work as a director, and Harold Lloyd to become a comedian with Mack Sennett's Keystone Company. But this was a temporary state of affairs for both of them.

In 1915, Hal Roach and his older brother, John B. Roach, set up the Hal Roach Studios on Santa Monica Boulevard in Los Angeles. Harold Lloyd was summoned back from Mack Sennett's two-reeler factory to become the studio's first comic actor. The brothers made the 'Lonesome Luke' series with Lloyd and got Pathé to distribute them. The films cost around $1200 each to make, but they brought the producers several times that amount in takings.

In 1919 they moved into a new studio at 8822 Washington Boulevard in Culver City, which became the Hal Roach Studios until 1959. What happened to John B. Roach after that is still uncertain: he disappears from *Who's Who in America* and the film histories mention only Hal Roach Sr and Hal Roach Jr.

Hal Roach assembled a large group of enthusiastic and experienced staff and paid them well. His studios were open six days a week, making what they described as 'slapstick with finesse'. During the first decade of operations, the studio gradually built up its own house style, and Hal Roach comedies looked better than anything produced by Mack Sennett or by companies such as Warner Brothers, Columbia, Fox and RKO, who made two-reel comedies to accompany features they had made themselves. But after a few years, Harold Lloyd moved to Pathé, which had now become Paramount. After ten years of distributing his films through Pathé, Roach found that MGM made an even better job of it. Mack Sennett, who was established well before Hal Roach began making films, told the *Motion Picture Herald* in an interview in 1930: 'Hal Roach is my only rival!' And indeed, his influence as 'The King of Comedy' waned as Hal Roach's became greater, to the point where Roach had a monopoly in the field. His distinctive touch was due partly to directors such as George Stevens, Leo and Ray McCarey, James and Charley Parrott (the latter better known as Charley Chase), James W. Horne, Gordon Douglas and Fred Guiol, to name but a few of the men who were able to develop their talents under the wing of Hal Roach.

Kelly the Second, (1936): Left to right: Guinn Williams, Patsy Kelly, Charley Chase.

Although the film world (or at least people in and around Hollywood) tended to look down on those who worked for Hal Roach, the latter often derived a great deal more satisfaction from their work than people on the payrolls of the big studios. When NBC interviewed a number of his former employees for a documentary, *The Film Factory*, they were unanimous in their memories of the place as

Some of the juvenile stars of the 'Our Gang' series which ran from 1922 to 1944. The line-up includes Pete the Wonderdog and, immediately to the right, Darla Hood and George 'Spanky' McFarland.

being one big, happy family, free from most of the normal hierarchies. Hal Roach was very much the boss, but he was a fair and respected employer. He would sometimes come down to the sets and take over directing the film for an hour or so, before moving on to the next one. People enjoyed working for him, and there was a lot of laughter involved.

Hal Roach's particular pet project was the 'Our Gang' series, a phenomenally successful series still sometimes shown on TV today under the new title of 'The Little Rascals'. From 1929 to 1944 he made 132 'Our Gang Talkie Shorts', although the series began with silent films in 1922. The best known of the many child stars used in the series was the already somewhat corpulent 'Spanky' McFarland, who played in ninety-five films between 1931 and 1942. He was three when his mother first entrusted him to the hands of the studio nanny, Mrs Carter. He took over the role of the departing 'Our Gang' fat boy, Joe Cobb, and was under contract to Hal Roach for the next eleven years.

The director of the first 'Our Gang' film was 'Uncle' Robert McGowan. Later, directors such as Gus Meins, Gordon Douglas and Fred Meyer were to record the exploits of the Gang on celluloid. All the films were supervised by Hal Roach; the scripts were written by H. M. Walker, and Stan Laurel often acted as adviser. Matthew Beard, who played the black boy Stymie in the series, told in a 1975 CBS documentary, 'Whatever Became of Hollywood?', how Spanky, Dickie Moore and he himself went to watch Stan and Oliver whenever they could. Matthew did an impression of Stan's cry-baby act, with his fingers pushed through his hair and Stan's bowler hat on his head. Hal Roach was not interested in Matthew's pranks, but Stan said, 'Hal, get the kid a derby. Make him happy!'

Hook and Ladder, (1932):
Second left: Stymie (Matthew Beard) with the hat he got from Stan Laurel.
Second from right: Spanky (George McFarland).

And from that moment on, Stymie wore a derby in the Our Gang films: it became his own trademark and a mark of respect to Stan Laurel. Matthew Beard's career was rather less of a success, though: he spent nine years in prison for handling and using drugs, and died in penury in 1982. He tells Anselma Dell'Olio in 'Whatever Became of Hollywood?': 'You know, it hurts to see yourself and The Little Rascals constantly on television and you don't get any money out of it'.

The same was also the case for Stan Laurel and Oliver Hardy and all the actors and actresses who worked for Roach. In the twenties and thirties television was a distant glint on the horizon, and work in the studio was fun. Hal Roach prospered, and so did his employees.

The extras in Hal Roach's films were often brothers and sisters, sons and daughters or husbands and wives of people working in the studio. If a dress or jacket got damaged, or clothes were needed that were not in the studio's enormous costumes department, Marguerite Roach would simply go into town and buy what was needed. The happy-go-lucky atmosphere at the studios was a major factor in Laurel and Hardy's success, and many other comedians got their careers off to a flying start in Culver City. But in 1935 and 1936, two-reelers became less popular, and Roach began making bigger-budgeted features and streamliners, halfway between a two-reeler and a feature in length and designed to whet the audience's appetite before a double bill.

Around this time, Roach also sold the rights to the Our Gang Comedies to MGM, who were now his distributors, and Monogram Pictures. Then, in 1938, he signed a contract with a new distributor: United Artists. In 1940, the fruitful relationship between Hal Roach and Laurel and Hardy came to an end. They had been working for him under separate contracts since 1926, and Stan Laurel in particular was beginning to get tired of this arrangement. He wanted Oliver Hardy and himself to sign up with Roach together as a team, but Roach refused for various reasons. Stan Laurel's contract expired in 1939, six months before that of Oliver Hardy. Hardy had to appear in one film with Harry Langdon as his new partner, *Zenophobia,* and then, when his contract ran out, Laurel and Hardy went off to work for the independent producer, Boris Morros, in *The Flying Deuces* (1939), a feature distributed by RKO Radio Pictures. In the spring of 1940, now under contract together rather than separately, they made two more films for Roach: *A Chump at Oxford* and *Saps at Sea.* After this, they went on to make eight feature films for 20th Century-Fox and MGM.

After Laurel and Hardy's departure, things began to go downhill somewhat. Five years earlier, one of Roach's comediennes, Thelma

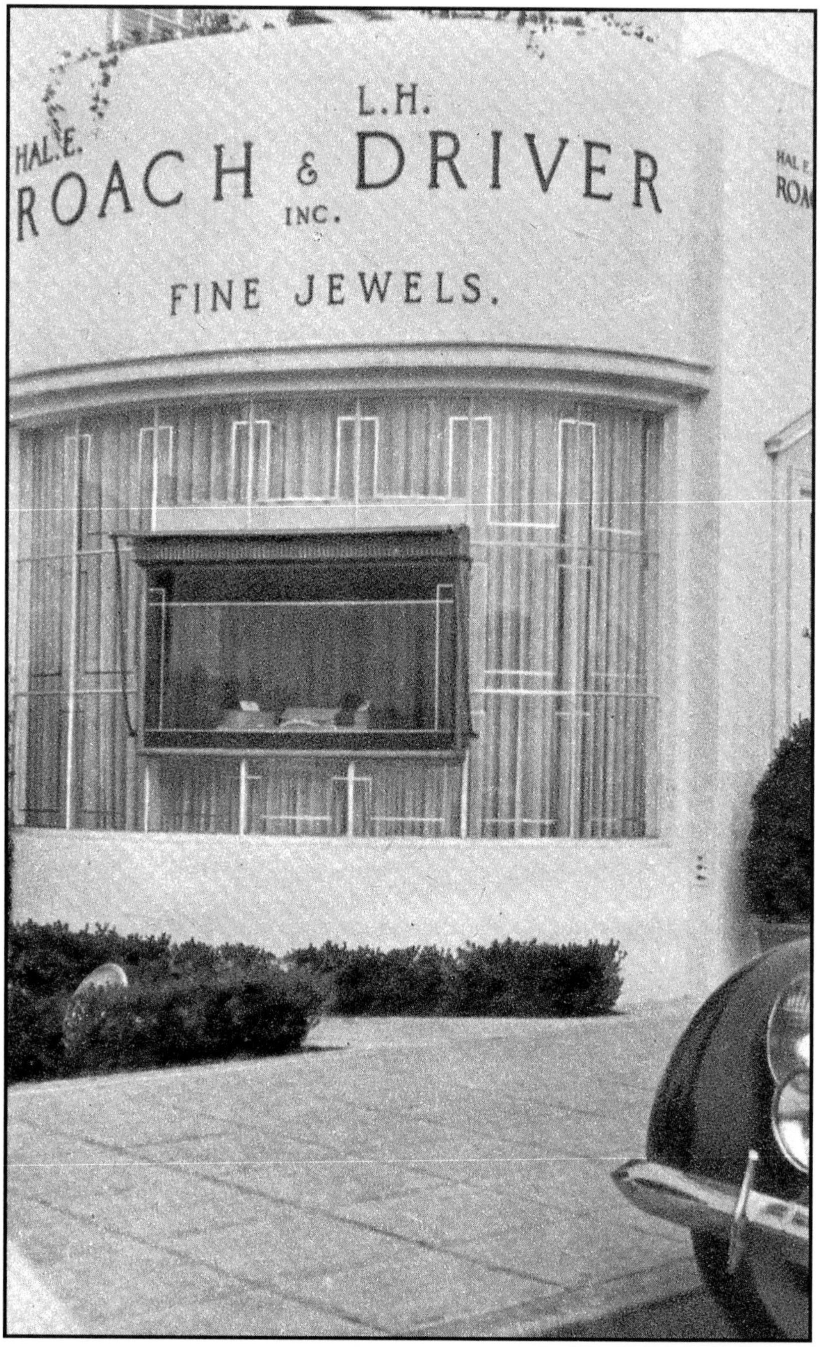

In the late 1930s, Hal Roach Sr was also involved in the diamond business: the shop he and his partner L.H. Driver owned in Beverly Hills.

Todd, 'The Icecream Blonde', had died, in suspicious circumstances, of carbon monoxide poisoning in her locked garage on the Pacific Highway between Santa Monica and Malibu. According to Kenneth Anger in *Hollywood Babylon* (Dell Publishing, New York, 1976), Mafia boss Lucky Luciano was not unconnected with her death. There are persistent rumours that Hal Roach himself was involved with the activities of the Mafia around this time, but the truth will probably never be known. Just before the outbreak of the Second World War, it is believed that work began in Hal Roach Studios on an anti-Fascist film, financed by a group of powerful Italian-American businessmen, with the intention of helping to bring about the fall of Benito Mussolini. No one has ever seen the result, assuming there was one. But it is known that in January 1942 the US Air Force took over the studios, with Roach's consent, and used them as a centre for making propaganda and training films. Military police kept guard at the entrance and soon Hal Roach Studios had been unofficially dubbed 'Fort Roach'. The crews wore uniforms, and the whole process was supervised by General H. H. Arnold of the Army Air Corps, who even gave Hal Roach the rank of Colonel in the Signal Corps.

Many actors did their 'military service' in Fort Roach, including William Holden, Edmond O'Brien, Van Heflin, Edgar Kennedy, George Montgomery and a certain Ronald Reagan.

In 1948, Hal Roach set up the Hal Roach Television Company and gradually sold the TV rights to his old two-reelers to various parties. In 1948 and 1949 he made his first feature films for television, *The Three Musketeers* and *Hurricane at Pilgrim Hill.* In 1955, Hal Roach Jr, then thirty-six, bought his father out for $10 million, thereby becoming America's foremost television film producer. The TV series he went on to make in the Old Hal Roach Studios from 1950 onwards fared well in the ratings. Local TV stations still show the odd few episodes from one now and then, usually at night or early in the morning. Some of Roach's

The Hal Roach Studios.

Sons of the Desert, (1933).

more popular TV series, all filmed in black-and-white in half-hour episodes, were 'Racket Squad' (98 episodes, CBS), 'Public Defender' (69 episodes, CBS), 'Trouble With Father' (130 episodes, ABC), 'My Little Margie' (126 episodes, NBC) and 'Passport to Danger' (30 episodes, CBS, with Steve McQueen in the starring role).

Hal Roach Sr, still a cheerful man who liked the odd flutter on the horses, and earned a living mass-producing comedies, had a number of setbacks in his personal life. He outlived his first wife Marguerite, who died in 1941, as well as his children Margaret (1921-64), Hal Jr (1919-72) and Elizabeth, his daughter, who lived only to the age of eight months. I am not certain whether his second wife, Lucille Prin, is still alive.

In 1959, the beautiful Old Hal Roach Studios were demolished in a single day. Since then, the land has been used for anything and everything, from car park to car wash to supermarket. At the end of 1984, 8822 Washington Boulevard housed a Nissan dealer; presumably by coincidence, one of the brands they sold was the Laurel.

The Music Box, (1932), which won Laurel and Hardy an Oscar.

Coo Coo (Ku Ku) the Laurel and Hardy Theme
A Musical Dialogue
Medium fast tempo
Play melody octave higher
legato
By T. MARVIN HATLEY
A. S. C. A. P.
Oliver Hardy
Piano
(loco)
Stan Laurel

7

T. Marvin Hatley: The unknown genius

We have already seen how warm and friendly the atmosphere at Hal Roach Studios on Washington Boulevard in Culver City was between 1930 and 1940. Many books written by people who knew or worked with Roach have recalled and emphasized this atmosphere.

T. Marvin Hatley, born in 1905 in Reed, Oklahoma, says in *Laurel and Hardy* by McCabe, Kilgore and Bann: 'A long time ago – those happy days. The Roach lot was a small one, and everybody knew and liked each other!' Hatley was the musical director of Hal Roach Studios and composer of the well-known Laurel and Hardy theme, the 'Cuckoo Song' (tum tum te tum, tum tum te tum). How this famous melody first came into being is uncertain, though we do know that in England Harry Steinberg wrote an arrangement of it which was performed as 'The Dance of the Cuckoos' by the London Symphony Orchestra conducted by Van Phillips. But the average Laurel and Hardy fan is not over-concerned with exactly how it originated, simply the fact that it exists.

Nevertheless, it would appear that he wrote it for a radio station owned by Warner Brothers which shared the studios with Hal Roach. Warner used it as an 'hour theme', a jingle broadcast every hour. Roach took it over from the radio station. In *Movie Mirror* (July 1933), Stan Laurel says the 'Cuckoo Song' was used for the beginning and end of a daily radio programme called 'The Cuckoo Hour'. According to Laurel, Oliver Hardy heard it and bought it from Marvin Hatley for $25.

And yet another version comes from Hatley himself. In an interview in *Screenland* for January 1947, he tells how one day in 1929 he was sitting at the piano in Hal Roach Studios improvising on the 'Cuckoo' theme, when along came Stan Laurel and asked him whether they could use a version of it as the Laurel and Hardy theme. This is also possible, for all their films from 1930 onwards, beginning with *Brats* and ending with their last short, *Thicker than Water* in 1935, were accompanied by Hatley's composition. Later the two-reelers that had originally been silent films were given a soundtrack by the distributors, and the tune was also used for these.

Marvin Hatley worked for Hal Roach for twelve years. The 'Cuckoo Song' was given the sub-title 'A Musical Dialogue' (Stan: *loco*; Oliver: *legato*). After writing the composition for Hal Roach, he gave up his job as a pianist for the radio station and became Roach's musical director. Hatley was a musician of long experience who could play a number of instruments faultlessly. At the studios, he was conductor of a studio orchestra, most of whose members were freelance. Hatley began writing incidental music for films, and also songs. Two of the best known, still popular today, are 'Honolulu Baby' from *Sons of the Desert* (1933) and 'Won't You Be My Lovely Dovety' from *Way Out West* (1937). For this, Marvin Hatley received an Oscar nomination, shared with LeRoy Shield, who often wrote music for Roach.

Brussels, Lido Palace, October 1947: Stan Laurel and Oliver Hardy meet the Dutch Deen Boyd Bachmann Orchestra.

The 'Our Gang' series, with Spanky and his 'little rascals', the Charley Chase shorts, and shorts and features starring Patsy Kelly and Thelma Todd (and, after Thelma's mysterious death, Patsy Kelly and Zasu Pitts), the 'Topper' series and any number of Laurel and Hardy films had their background music composed by Hatley.

Like the films, the music still retains its popularity to this day, and the 'Laurel and Hardy' record from a series produced by United Artists called 'The Golden Age of Hollywood' was a best-seller. Apart from

Saps at Sea, (1940): The last film Laurel and Hardy made for Hal Roach, and not their best.

original work by Hatley, this includes the cowboy song which Laurel and Hardy sing in *Way Out West.* With Stan's part sung by Chill Wills, this song made a brief re-appearance as 'The Trail of the Lonesome Pine' in the British charts in 1976, nearly forty years after its première. 'The Trail of the Lonesome Pine' was by Harry Carroll and Ballard MacDonald, with Marvin Hatley conducting the studio orchestra.

During breaks in filming at Hal Roach Studios, Stan Laurel and Marvin Hatley, now the firmest of friends, used to enjoy spells of musical clowning, with Hatley on the piano and Stan singing English music-hall songs. Laurel himself was a good accordion player, but that was the limit of his musical skills. If Stan had to play any other instrument in one of his films, Marvin Hatley would have to show him how to hold it and make it look as though he had been playing it all his life. When Stan plays the tuba in *Swiss Miss* (1939) to accompany Oliver as he serenades his beloved Anna under her window, it is actually Marvin Hatley playing off-screen as Oliver sings (he had a good singing voice) 'Let me call you sweetheart, I'm in love with you!' The same thing happens in *Saps at Sea* from 1940, only this time it is the trombone which Stan is pretending to play. Marvin Hatley is still alive: vigorous, cheerful, and eighty years old, the great man of film music lives in Hollywood Hills and pursues his hobby of gardening.

Swiss Miss, (1938).

the San Fernando Valley during the 1930s was William Claude Dukenfield, better known as W. C. Fields. Stan Laurel often joined in too, and both agreed that Fields was 'one of the most naturally funny men'. And half a century later, many people still agree with them. But both in and out of the studios, Fields did very little to make himself popular as a person. His verbal aggression is still legendary: with his nasal, drink-sodden tones and red nose he would hurl invective in all directions, and he took pleasure in preserving his image as a hater of children and dogs (Do you like children? Fields: Sure! As long as they're well-cooked!) But when he died on Christmas Day 1946, aged

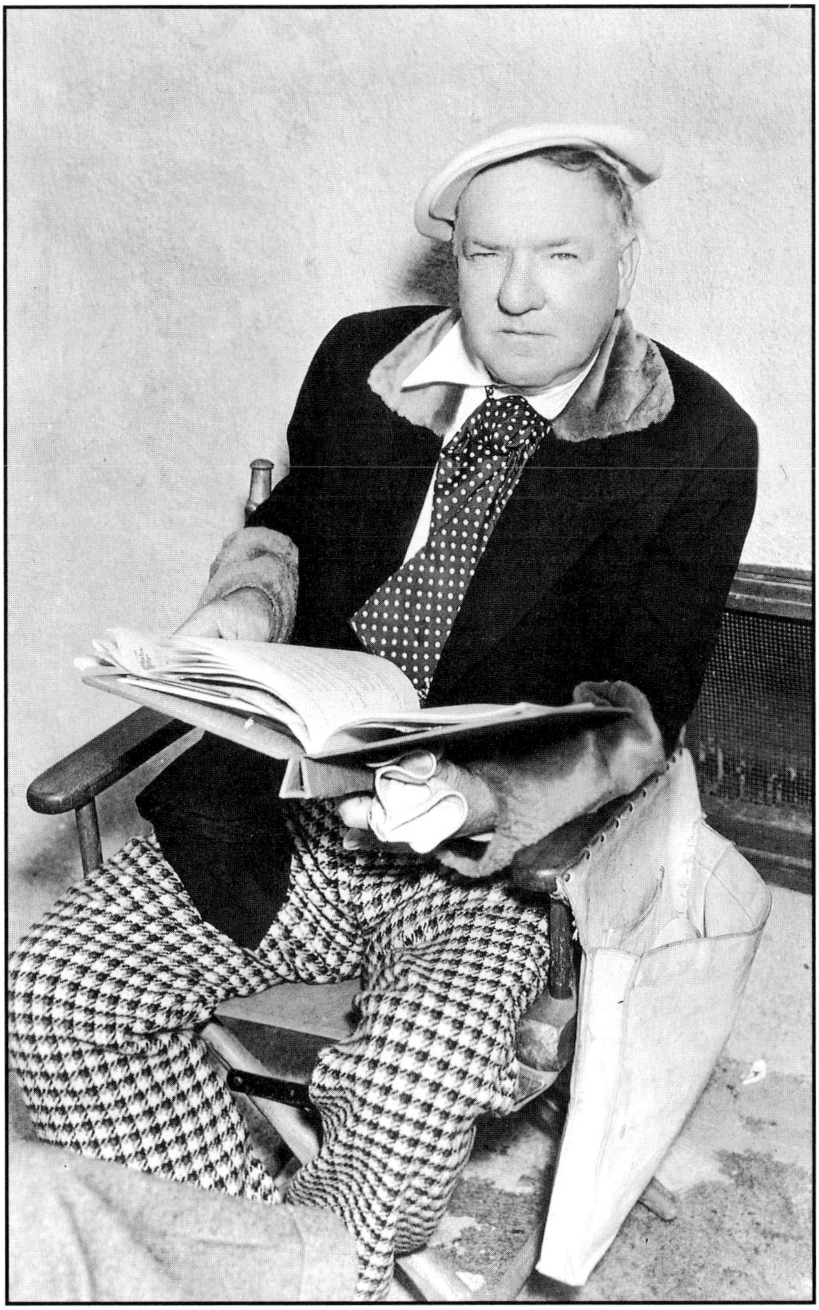

Poppy, (1936): W.C. Fields.

sixty-seven, he left upwards of $1 million to an orphanage. Some of the sayings ascribed to Fields have passed into legend, such as his assertion that 'Women are like elephants to me – I like to look at them, but I wouldn't want to own one!' and 'Any man who hates small dogs and children can't be all bad!' His sometimes rough-edged humour, which he directed against bureaucracy and convention, still has a strong appeal to film-goers today. His films are often shown on television in America and elsewhere, and they are still capable of filling a cinema.

In 1979, the hundredth anniversary of Fields' birth, the American Post Office issued a particularly attractive 15¢ stamp portraying the great comedian. This was the culmination of thirteen years of efforts by the W. C. Fields Fan Club to get a postage stamp honouring the great comedian. At the time of writing, the Sons of the Desert, Laurel and Hardy's fan club, are still pestering the US authorities for a similar stamp to commemorate their idols.

W. C. Fields made a number of silent films, but it was not until sound arrived on the scene that his talents came to fruition. It was between 1932 and 1942 that he produced his best work, often making use of his consummate talent for juggling and conjuring. Another distinctive feature of Fields' comedies in comparison with others of the time was their lack of pathos and their frequently expressed hatred of mankind. He continually drew inspiration from his negative view of the world, and it is not hard to pad out books and articles about Fields using adjectives such as incomprehensible, ironic, aggressive, melancholic, gruff, cynical, embittered. Fields often wrote the scripts for his films under pseudonyms such as Mahatma Kane Jeeves, Otis J. Criblecoblis and Charles Bogle (*Bank Dick*, 1940; *Never Give a Sucker an Even Break*, 1941; *You Can't Cheat an Honest Man*, 1939). In all, his work consists of thirty-four feature films and five shorts, *The Golf Specialist* (RKO, 1930), *The Dentist* (Paramount-Sennett, 1932), *The Fatal Glass of Beer* (Paramount-Sennett, 1933), *The Pharmacist* (Paramount-Sennett, 1933) and *The Barber Shop* (Paramount-Sennett, 1933).

Of all Laurel and Hardy's competitors in the field of screen comedy, the greatest was Charles Chaplin, formerly a friend and colleague of Stan Laurel in England and for a few years after they both arrived in the United States. No comedian has had more said or written about him than Charles Chaplin. In 1910, when American film comedy was still in its infancy and circus and variety artistes were starting to beat a path to the film studios, there was already the beginnings of a comic tradition in film in Europe. Many Americans were inspired by the French comedian Max Linder, whilst Lumière's short comedy, *L'Arroseur Arrosé* was gratuitously copied by many American film-makers. And as early as 1898, the British film pioneer, Arthur Melbourne Cooper, was putting comic chase scenes in his films. But in the United States, the genre still had a lot of catching up to do.

Before 1913, the American slapstick industry was still only beginning to discover the multitude of possibilities film offered for everything that

The Kid, (1921): Charlie Chaplin, Jackie Coogan and Tom Wilson as the policeman.

was fast-moving, rough and spectacular. They aimed fairly and squarely at Joe Public, for entertainment for the upper classes still consisted of theatre- and concert-going, and they tended to look down on the cinema.

In amongst all the tumult of custard-pie throwing and falling over, there came a new type of comedy. The man responsible for it was formerly a member of Fred Karno's troupe of British music-hall entertainers who was taken on by Mack Sennett as a film comedian in 1913 for $125 dollars. His name was Charles Chaplin.

Chaplin was born in Victorian London in 1889, the son of another artiste, Hannah Hill. He took his own particular style and experience with him to America, where this form of pantomime was almost unheard-of in Mack Sennett's Keystone Studios. But Chaplin introduced a slower, more sedate form of acting, and became a kind of teacher for his new colleagues.

Chaplin had had a poverty-stricken, almost Dickensian upbringing. In *The Kid* (1920), with tiny Jackie Coogan at his side, he conveys something of the Oliver Twist existence to his audience, and sixty years after it was made it is still a beautiful and powerfully evocative film. Apart from Keystone Studios, Chaplin also worked for Essanay, Mutual, First National and finally for his own company, United Artists, which he set up in 1919 with Douglas Fairbanks, Mary Pickford and D. W. Griffith. Chaplin's leading lady in thirty-five of his films was Edna Purviance. It was the figure of the Tramp which made Chaplin famous throughout the world, and he played this character for over twenty-two years. It was not until 1940, with *The Great Dictator,* that he finally abandoned the bowler hat and tails. Chaplin died on 25 December 1977, aged eighty-nine, in his house in Vevey on Lake Geneva. His wife Oona was by his side. Chaplin began life on the wrong footing, with his early years spent in poverty, but the major part of his life was prosperous and varied. He rubbed shoulders with such famous personalities as Einstein, Toscanini, Shaw, Picasso, Gandhi and Churchill. The Queen knighted him and Oxford University gave him an honorary doctorate. Any of the large number of books published about the great little man will give a list of the films he made.

Sherlock Jr, (1924): Buster Keaton.

Buster Keaton, like Stan Laurel, had been in the theatre almost since he learned to walk. At the turn of the century Joseph Francis Keaton was five and his mother was sewing a handle to her son's jacket so that his father could hurl him into the wings or against the curtain at the back of the stage as part of their act, The Three Keatons. Whilst still little more than an infant he would be thrown around the stage in a manner which would have the NSPCC up in arms if it happened today. His nickname came from Harry Houdini, who once said of one of Keaton's tumbles: 'That's some buster your baby took!'

The height of Buster Keaton's career was before the arrival of the sound film. His later films are far less technically accomplished and less humorous as well. His trademark was the fact that no matter what happened, no matter how great the adversity besetting him, he never showed any expression on film. Stan Laurel was a great admirer of his, and this respect was mutual. After Stan Laurel was cremated, Keaton said in the Church of the Hollywood Hills: 'Stan was the greatest. Even greater than Chaplin, Charlie was second. And don't let anyone fool you about that.' Only three weeks before he died, Keaton had been to see him in his flat in Santa Monica, and these two great cinematic geniuses, two of history's most famous clowns, spent three hours talking about show business. To say the least, its a pity no one was there with a tape recorder.

At the end of 1965, three months before he died on 1 February 1966, Buster Keaton received a standing ovation at the Venice Film Festival, apparently emotionless. The auditorium full of great film-makers applauded loud and long the man to whom so many of them owed so much. His films cover the period from 1917 (when he was making comedies with Roscoe 'Fatty' Arbuckle) until 1967, after he died when *War Italian Style* first came out. In 1957, Daniel Petrie made *The Buster Keaton Story* with Donald O'Connor as a lacklustre version of Keaton. A better tribute was *Four Clowns,* a Robert Youngson compilation made in 1970 which includes extracts from Buster Keaton's 1925 film, *Seven Chances.* And there are a multitude of books about Keaton available in any specialist bookshop.

For thirty years, from 1930 to 1960, a trio of aggressive humorists kept their worldwide audiences in stitches. They have also enjoyed a minor revival on television where, in the United States at least, their films make fairly frequent appearances. The Stooges' speciality is a kind of pitilessly violent slapstick, sometimes not unlike Tom and Jerry. Skulls are cracked, eyes poked and shins kicked with almost monotonous regularity. The physical violence is accompanied by exaggeratedly loud bangs from the sound-effects man.

Most of The Three Stooges' two-reelers were made in Harry Cohn's slightly upmarket B-movie studio at Columbia. There is one thing nobody could accuse their shorts of being, and that is boring, The trio are constantly in motion, and the films are not unlike Mack Sennett's

The Three Stooges, (1945).

early comedies with their frenetic pace, except that in The Three Stooges' case the action is accompanied by noise. The original Stooges (although there were many changes of personnel during their history) were Moe Howard (1895-1975), his brother Shemp Howard (1900-55) and Larry Fine (1911-74). The trio made up the longest running comedy series in film history, and amongst those who directed them were Leo McCarey, Charley Chase, Jules White and Edward Bernds. In 1934 they were directed by Ray McCarey in *Men in Black* and *Three Little Pigskins*; two years previously, he had directed Laurel and Hardy for Hal Roach in *Scram!* and *Pack Up Your Troubles.*

The Three Stooges were geniuses in their field as well as being the longest active on the screen of any of their competitors. But although there is still a good deal of demand for their films, they are an acquired taste. Half the people that watch them are likely to fall off their seats with laughter, but the other half will be hard put to find anything funny amongst all this violent slapstick. In America they were hailed as true artists: 'The wildest trio in the history of American entertainment, the most popular film comedy team in show business!' In 1934 the Stooges (Moe Howard, Curly Howard and Larry Fine) appeared in an MGM film, made partly in colour, called *Hollywood Party*; Laurel and Hardy also played in the film.

In October 1969, Groucho Marx committed a motoring offence in Madison and a policeman stopped him. He asked to see Groucho's licence, looked at it, and then said 'What? You're Groucho Marx?

At the Circus, (1939): Groucho and Chico Marx.

Forget about the ticket I was going to give you! But I want to ask you one thing – why aren't there more Laurel and Hardy movies on television?'

Groucho Marx was the oldest of the five Marx Brothers, and died in August 1977. He was preceded by his brothers Chico, Harpo and Gummo, who died in 1961, 1964 and 1977 respectively, whilst Zeppo died at the end of November 1979.

The best-known of the brothers in their films were Groucho, Harpo (who never once opens his mouth) and the Victor Borge-like piano virtuoso, Chico. Gummo did not make a career in films, and Zeppo is a less distinctive figure than the other brothers. But the main source of humour in all the films is Groucho, with his venomous strings of insults to all and sundry and his huge fake moustache. Groucho retained his bizarre sense of humour long after he stopped making films, unleashing his sarcastic wisecracks on everyone he met. When he was eighty-five he still had a girlfriend, Erin Fleming, who was very much younger than himself. He told reporters with his usual sly grin: 'My relationship with Erin is purely physical!'

The Marx Brothers' best-known films were:

The Cocoanuts, Paramount, 1929
Animal Crackers, Paramount, 1930
Monkey Business, Paramount, 1931
Horse Feathers, Paramount, 1932
Duck Soup, Paramount, 1932
A Night at the Opera, MGM, 1935
A Day at the Races, MGM, 1937
Room Service, RKO, 1938
At the Circus, MGM, 1939
Go West, MGM, 1940
The Big Store, MGM, 1941
A Night in Casablanca, United Artists, 1946

After Laurel and Hardy, Bud Abbott (1895-1974) and Lou Costello (1906-59) were the best-known duo in the comedy business. Lou was the small fat man of the two, Bud the dapper 'straight man' in a suit who fed Lou his lines. When they signed their contract with Universal International they had already established a reputation on the radio. They made their film début in 1940 in *One Night in the Tropics,* directed by A. Edward Sutherland, who had worked with Chaplin in *A Woman of Paris* (1923) and directed the Laurel and Hardy feature, *The Flying Deuces* (1939, RKO). As Laurel and Hardy's popularity gradually waned, so Abbott and Costello moved to take their place, despite the fact that Laurel and Hardy were a far superior comedy team. But *One Night in the Tropics* was a huge success and thirty-seven Abbott and Costello films followed in quick succession.

Abbott and Costello both grew up in the tradition of American burlesque and this style shows through in the humour of their films. In fact, their films were well-made, unpretentious B-movies, but they are totally without the charm and warmth of Laurel and Hardy in their best films. They simply do their best to amuse the audience as much as possible using their technique of high-speed cross-talk, a technique which they had honed to perfection. A particularly famous example is their 'Who's on First' sketch, which revolves around the names of the players in a baseball team. In their fourteenth film, *The Naughty Nineties,* they were still doing this routine despite having used it any number of times in nightclubs and on radio, but it still works. If you listen very closely to the soundtrack, you can actually hear muffled laughter from the studio crew. The laughter it provokes has none of the subtlety that the best of today's comedies can provoke. It is a far less sophisticated humour, but humour nevertheless. Director Jean Yarbrough deliberately allowed the unscripted laughter to remain in the film, which caused him problems later on. In an interview with Howard Waldorf in the *Post-Enquirer* in December 1946, he tells how he was carpeted by Universal's Production Manager, Martin Murphy, for doing so.

'Who's on First' is a variant on the 'How High is a Chinaman' theme; here, Abbott and Costello are discussing the three baseball players, Who, What and I-Don't-Know.

Bud: I say Who's on first, What's on second, I-Don't-Know's on third.
Lou: Yeah, you know the fellow's name?
Bud: Yes!
Lou: Well, who's on first?
Bud: Yes.
Lou: I mean the fellow's name.
Bud: Yes.
Lou: I mean the guy playing first.
Bud: Who!
Lou: The fellow playing first.
Bud: Who.
Lou: The first baseman.
Bud: Who!
Lou: The guy playing first.
Bud: Who's on first!
Lou: Well, what are you asking me for?

Like the good 'feeder' that he is, Lou Costello is able to persuade his small, naive partner that he is not actually standing where he is:

Lou: Are you in St Louis?
Bud: No.
Lou: Are you in Chicago?
Bud: Of course not!
Lou: Well, if you're not in St Louis and you're not in Chicago, you must be somewhere else.
Bud: Eh, Ye-es...
Lou: Well then, if you're somewhere else, you're not here!

Whilst they were still busy on their thirty-second film, *Abbot and Costello go to Mars,* which they made with Universal in 1953, they also made their television début on the CBS network in 'The Abbot and Costello Show', which eventually ran to fifty-two episodes. The series was directed by Jean Yarbrough and the thirty-minute programmes received an enthusiastic welcome from the public. Vaudeville, radio, cabaret, film and now television: Abbot and Costello had done them all. But in 1957, this famous team went their own separate ways. It is not unlikely that, just as happened with Laurel and Hardy, there will be a revival of Abbot and Costello's films on television. The best of their

Africa Screams, (1949): Bud Abbott and Lou Costello.

films are around forty years old, and watching them can be a nostalgic experience. They are still shown in the United States, as are episodes of the TV series. Bill Hanna and Joe Barbera, who earlier had made Tom and Jerry cartoons for MGM and then 'The Flintstones' for Screen Gems, produced 156 five-minute Abbot and Costello cartoons between 1966 and 1972. Bud Abbot's voice was used for his cartoon equivalent, whilst Stan Irwin played Lou Costello. Cartoon versions of Laurel and Hardy have also been made, produced for TV in 1966 by Larry Harmon (Stan's voice is done by John McGeorge, and Oliver's by Larry Harmon, the man beind 'The Laurel and Hardy Cartoon Show').

These were the films Abbott and Costello made:

One Night in the Tropics, Universal, 1940
Buck Privates, Universal, 1941
In the Navy, Universal, 1941
Hold that Ghost, Universal, 1941
Keep 'Em Flying, Universal, 1941
Ride 'Em Cowboy, Universal, 1942
Rio Rita, Universal, 1942
Pardon my Sarong, Universal 1942
Who Done It?, Universal 1942
It Ain't Hay, Universal, 1942
Hit the Ice, Universal, 1943

The Wistful Widow of Wagon Gap, (1947): Bud Abbott and Lou Costello.

In Society, Universal, 1944
Lost in a Harem, MGM, 1944
The Naughty Nineties, Universal, 1945
Abbott and Costello in Hollywood, MGM, 1945
Here Come the Co-Eds, Universal, 1945
Little Giant, Universal, 1946
The Time of Their Lives, Universal, 1946
Buck Privates Come Home, Universal, 1947
The Wistful Widow of Wagon Gap, Universal, 1947
The Noose Hangs High, Eagle-Lion, 1948
Abbott and Costello Meet Frankenstein, Universal, 1948
Mexican Hayride, Universal, 1948
Abbott and Costello Meet the Killer: Boris Karloff, Universal, 1949
Africa Screams, United Artists, 1949
Abbott and Costello in the Foreign Legion, Universal, 1950
Abbott and Costello Meet the Invisible Man, Universal, 1951
Comin' Round the Mountain, Universal, 1951
Jack and the Beanstalk, Warner Brothers, 1952
Lost in Alaska, Universal, 1952
Abbott and Costello Meet Captain Kidd, Warner Brothers, 1952
News of the Day, MGM, 1952 (guest appearance in newsreel)
Abbott and Costello Go to Mars, Universal, 1953
Abbott and Costello Meet Dr Jekyll and Mr Hyde, Universal, 1953
Hollywood Grows Up, Columbia, 1954 (guest appearance in Screen Snapshots)
Abbott and Costello Meet the Keystone Cops, Universal, 1955
Abbott and Costello Meet the Mummy, Universal, 1955
Dance with Me Henry, United Artists, 1956
The World of Abbott and Costello, Universal, 1965 (compilation)

In the 1950s, the dynamic duo of Dean Martin and Jerry Lewis set their seal on American film comedy. Dean Martin (born on 17 June 1917 as Dino Paul Crocetti) and Jerry Lewis (16 March 1929 as Joseph Levitch) made seventeen films for Paramount between 1949 and 1956, and also appeared in a short for Columbia in 1952, *Hollywood Fun Festival.* After these comedies, Martin and Lewis split up and each took his own separate direction in the entertainment industry. Jerry Lewis made himself a name as a director, ideas man, writer, producer and solo comedian. He also worked lecturing in academies and film workshops. He was especially highly regarded in France where the very highbrow film journal, *Cahiers du Cinéma* praised him for his originality and insight as a film-maker, and where some famous young directors were well-nigh fanatical about Jerry.

Looking at the Martin and Lewis comedies now, it is easy to see why between 1950 and 1960 they were regarded as America's foremost film comedians. Some of their fast-paced, only semi-scripted repartee is memorably good. The feeder of the two, Dean Martin (it was often said at the time that he would have been nothing without Jerry Lewis), in fact went on to become a moderately good film actor (*Rio Bravo* in 1959, *Sergeants Three* in 1962, *Four for Texas* in 1963 and *Bandolero* in 1968 were examples of his work). Dean Martin also demonstrated his great talents for spontaneous humour and perfect timing for nine years from 1965 to 1975 in 'The Dean Martin Show', broadcast with great success by NBC. In December 1978, *Esquire* magazine published an article about Martin and Lewis by director/scriptwriter Peter Bogdanovich in which Martin tells how Frank Sinatra had them as guests on a live TV show and at a certain point sent Jerry Lewis off with an exaggeratedly imperious gesture so that he and Dean could sing a duet together. This he did, and Dean Martin punctuated the live

The Caddy, (1953): Dean Martin, Norman Taurog (director) and Jerry Lewis.

performance in the same light-hearted manner Jerry Lewis had done in the Martin and Lewis films. He deliberately walked off camera, said stupid things, pretended to trip over, made comments to members of the orchestra and made very sure that Jerry Lewis was seeing all this. Which Lewis did, looking dourly on. The one thing that was very clear from this programme was that Dean Martin had obtained his revenge, and from then on, whenever any mention was made of Martin and Lewis as a comedy team, Dean Martin was seen as the true comedian and Jerry Lewis as the 'straight man'.

Despite this, Stan Laurel was a great admirer of Jerry Lewis, and the respect was mutual. But Stan Laurel had trouble really appreciating Jerry Lewis's humour: he thought it was too chaotic, too unsubtle and too little thought out. After Oliver Hardy died, Jerry Lewis offered Stan Laurel a generous fee to come and write gags for him and to go through the scripts for his films and edit or add to them. But Stan Laurel declined, politely giving as the reason the fact that he valued his friendship with Lewis more than the idea of their working together in partnership. He was also being faithful to the memory of Oliver Hardy: he did not want to work with anyone else after his partner died.

Jerry Lewis, who by now had become a mega-personality, paid a great deal of attention to Laurel and Hardy's films. He thought nothing of lifting whole scenes from their films and using them little disguised in his own. In *The Sad Sack,* for example, he empties a tipper truck full of sand into an open jeep, exactly as Stan Laurel had done in *Blockheads* in 1938. There is insufficient room to give other examples of how Jerry Lewis was 'inspired' by Laurel and Hardy's films, but there are very many of them.

These were the films Dean Martin and Jerry Lewis made together, all with Paramount Pictures:

My Friend Irma, 1949
My Friend Irma Goes West, 1950
At War with the Army, 1950
That's My Boy, 1951
Sailor Beware, 1951
Jumping Jacks, 1952
Road to Bali, 1952 (guest appearance)
The Stooge, 1953
Scared Stiff, 1953
The Caddy, 1953
Money From Home, 1953
Living It Up, 1954
Three-Ring Circus, 1954
You're Never Too Young, 1955
Artists and Models, 1955
Pardners, 1956
Hollywood or Bust, 1956
Hollywood Fun Festival (Columbia short), 1952

9

Two Men, No Brains

Stan Laurel and Oliver Hardy may no longer be with us, but their films live on. Altogether they made 81 shorts and 24 feature films, all of them varying between funny and very funny. It is difficult to find anyone who does not experience some sort of pleasure at a Laurel and Hardy film. Charlie Chaplin may be funny, W.C. Fields even funnier, and Woody Allen a master of modern humour, but I think Laurel and Hardy outdo them all.

The true Laurel and Hardy fan has to grasp every available opportunity to see films made by the duo. Although ever since the 1960s there have been a good twenty books written about them in English alone, it would seem that the more often the work of a film actor or director is written about in books, the less his or her work is seen being shown in public. This is very true of Laurel and Hardy: a conclusion I have reached based on my own experience of years spent watching their films with a great deal of pleasure. But even for someone less enthusiastic than myself, it can still be quite a job to see their films on any kind of regular basis, either in the cinema, on TV, on video or in private showings by archives and museums. With a bit of luck you could see one Laurel and Hardy a month via one medium or another. In the cinema alone, this is no longer possible.

Books about Laurel and Hardy are a reasonable substitute, particularly if they contain some good photographs. Stills have a great deal of attraction for their nostalgia value but of course they can never give the same pure pleasure that the viewing of a film can. Nor can the mere recounting of scenes do much towards creating that 'do you remember' feeling.

Nevertheless, the better the comedian, the harder it is to avoid doing this. Take *Below Zero* (1930) for example. The film was directed by

Below Zero, (1930): Laurel and Hardy trying to earn a crust as street musicians.

James Parrott, with George Stevens behind the camera and editor Richard Currey. The opening titles: 'The freezing winter of 1929 will long be remembered: Mr Hardy's nose was so blue, Mr Laurel shot it for a jay-bird!'

Laurel and Hardy are playing a double bass and a harmonium in a blizzard-swept, almost deserted street. The tune is 'In the good old summertime'. Oliver plays the double bass and sings; at the end of the verse, a snowball hits him full in the face in close-up. As the melting snow drips slowly off his cheeks and nose, a snarling voice off-camera growls: 'In the good old summertime...' Charlie Hall is trying to scrape the hard frozen snow off the pavement with a coal shovel, or so it would appear from the soundtrack. He is irritated by Laurel and Hardy's choice of music, not least because he is close to catching his death of cold, and it is he who has thrown the missile. Oliver's first instinct is to attack him, but he is prevented from wreaking his revenge by Stan, who sits behind the harmonium and says to his fellow-musician: 'Ignore him. Just one of the lower elements!'

Oliver Hardy thinks for a moment, nods in agreement, taps his hat over to one side and the two continue their concert. The snow falls even harder. Charlie Hall bends down to pick up another snowball, then thinks better of it, shrugs and walks off with his spade.

Earlier, a woman opens a window on the first floor of a house and calls: 'Yoohoo, Mr Whiteman!' Oliver, polite as ever, doffs his hat and says: 'Yes, ma'am?' The woman wants to know how much money they earn for each street they play in. The pair stand there in the snow, pondering, the camera viewing them from overhead from the viewpoint of the woman. 'I would say about fifty cents a street', says Oliver, after a certain amount of counting on his fingers. The women reaches into her purse, throws something down to them with a nonchalant gesture and says in a friendly manner, as though she were talking to someone who was not quite all there, 'There's a dollar – move down a couple of streets!'

It is not exactly a tribute to their musical talents, but they have made something out of it. Then something falls into their collecting tin with an audible clang. Oliver is the first to get there, snatches it and looks into it. His sad gaze moves slowly round to the camera, Stan looks into the tin and sees that it is an egg. The pigeon that laid it is on the edge of a window-frame. Stan hurls a snowball at the unfortunate bird, and with the usual perfect timing of a Laurel and Hardy film, a man leans out of the window at precisely the wrong moment and is hit on the forehead by the snowball. He throws another one back at them, with more force than accuracy, and it lands with a plop in a bucket of milk being carried by a tall woman who is about to go into her house. The thrower of the snowball hurriedly withdraws: he recognizes the woman as one of his neighbours. She walks slowly up to Oliver Hardy and attacks him as he lamely carries on plucking on his double bass. Stan grabs her bucket and throws the contents onto the street as though it were dirty washing-up water. Oliver laughs uproariously, slapping his knees with pleasure and pointing to the empty bucket and the wet patch on the pavement. His pleasure is short-lived. The woman picks up the double bass as Stan and Oliver look on in fascination, and smashes the instrument over Oliver Hardy's head. It looks painful: even though it may only be a cardboard prop, she hits him pretty hard.

The second part of *Below Zero* is also worthy of description. The dream of every big-city pauper comes true: Laurel and Hardy find a wallet full of money lying in the street. In their exuberance, they invite a policeman (Frank Holiday) to join them for a bite in Pete's for Eats. Pete, the owner, is played by Stanley Sandford. Oliver Hardy has been transformed by the windfall: he is now a suave, debonair man about town. Sitting with the policeman at a round table with a check tablecloth, *garçon* Pete, the policeman, man of means Oliver and a highly cheerful Stan have the following conversation.

Pete: Now, what are you boys going to have?
Oliver: What about a large juicy steak, officer?
Policeman: That sounds good to me.
Oliver: Three great big steaks, smothered in onions!
Pete: Yes, sir!

Oliver:	And don't forget – plenty of onions!
Pete:	Yes, sir!
Oliver:	Oh *garçon*... bring me a *parfait.*
Pete:	Yes, sir.
Stan:	Put one on my steak too!
Oliver:	You don't put *parfaits* on steaks... Just cancel the *parfaits*!
Pete:	Yes, sir.
Oliver:	But bring me a small *demi-tasse.*
Pete:	Yes, sir.
Stan:	Oh, Geston!
Pete:	Yes, sir.
Stan:	Bring me one too – in a big cup!
Oliver:	A big cup. Where were you brung up? You pardon my friend's ignorance.

The feast comes to an abrupt end when it turns out that the policeman is the owner of the wallet they have found. He pays for his share and leaves his benefactors without a cent to their names. The situation bodes somewhat ill for Stan and Oliver, for we have already seen how Pete and his cronies deal with people who can't pay their bills.

Below Zero, (1930): Stan has been thrown out of a café into a barrel of water, so he drinks it dry.

The Fixer Uppers, (1935): Laurel and Hardy and the Hal Roach Studios' *House drunkard*, Arthur Housman.

In another establishment, the Café des Artistes, Laurel and Hardy are greetings-card salesmen waiting for Pierre Gustave (the sinister Charles Middleton), who has challenged Oliver Hardy to a duel. They sit at a table with the same chequered tablecloth as that in Pete's for Eats. The phone rings and Stan grabs the receiver and says after a moment: 'It sure is!' Asks Oliver: 'Who was that?'

Stan: Oh, some fellow havin' a joke.
Oliver: What did he say?
Stan: Well, I said, 'Hello', and the fellow said: 'It's a long distance from Atlanta, Georgia', and I said: 'Sure it is.' Silliest thing I ever...
Oliver: I wish there was some way to put a stop to those practical jokers!

The Fixer Uppers (1935, directed by Charles Rogers) is not generally regarded as a particularly good Laurel and Hardy two-reeler. But the acting is superb (with Charles Middleton as the artist Gustave, Mae Busch as Gustave's wife and Arthur Housman as a hospitable drunkard), the storyline is a good one and the scripts of a very high standard. Their package of greeting cards includes an all-purpose one:

A Merry Christmas, husband
Happy New Year's nigh.
I wish you Easter Greetings
Hooray for the Fourth of July!

One of their first customers is the alcoholic Housman, who is bowled over by Stan's work of genius on a Christmas card (read out in dramatic tones by Oliver Hardy):

Merry Christmas, Mother,
Merry Christmas, Ma.
Hi, Mommy, Mommy,
And a hot cha cha!

But Mrs Gustave does not need one of their cards. What she wants is someone to make her husband jealous. Oliver Hardy is quite happy to do this for $50. She shows Oliver how she gets her husband worked up: Stan acts as the guinea pig for a kiss which looks as though it will never come to an end, although it only lasts fifty seconds on film Stan keeps his hat and gloves on for the duration. Oliver Hardy watches, not a little perplexed, then starts getting bored, looks at his watch, listens to see whether it is still working, and nods in the affirmative to the camera. Finally he interrupts the kiss simply by tapping Mae Busch's bare shoulder. She turns round and Stan falls exhausted to the floor, but quickly gets to his feet and prepares to start anew. But now it is Oliver's turn to put into practice what he has just learned: their lips have been touching for barely a second, he sighs deeply, and the master of the house comes in. All hell breaks loose, and the artist demands satisfaction in the form of a duel.

In Laurel and Hardy's world, it is logical that if Oliver decides to exchange the temporal existence for the eternal, Stan should follow him. Oliver has decided to commit suicide by throwing himself into the Seine with a stone tied round his waist. The scene takes place in their feature film, *The Flying Deuces* (1939, directed by A. Edward Sutherland), and a lost love is the reason for Oliver's act of despair. Stan actually has no wish to enter the hereafter, but Oliver persuades him that life without Oliver will be unbearable.

> Oliver: So that's the kind of guy you are. After all I've done for you! Do you realize that after I'm gone you'll just go on living by yourself? People would stare at you and wonder what you are. And I wouldn't be there to *tell* them! They'd be no one to protect you. Do you want that to happen to *you*?

Stan is embarrassed. He puts on his I'm-about-to-cry face and says: 'I never thought of that...I'm sorry if I hurt your feelings, Oliver...I didn't mean to be so impolite...

Not that Stan is always such a softy in Oliver Hardy's presence. In their two-reel *Helpmates* (1931, directed by James Parrott), Stan snarls to Oliver in the kitchen: 'Say, who do you think I am, Cinderella? You know, if I had any sense, I'd leave!' Oliver: 'Well, it's a good thing you haven't!'

The introductory titles of *Helpmates* read: 'When the cat's away – the mice start looking up telephone numbers!' Then we see Oliver Hardy talking to himself in the mirror. He organized a wild party the previous night. His one-sided conversation is interrupted by the doorbell: it is a telegram, telling him that Mrs Hardy is planning to arrive at nine o'clock, and the apartment still looks as though an orgy has taken place. In panic, he phones Stan.

The Fixer Uppers, (1935): with Mae Busch in the forty-four-second kiss.

Stan: Hello?
Oliver: Where have you been?
Stan: I was here, with me.
Oliver: Why weren't you at the party last night?
Stan: I couldn't make it. I was bitten by a dog.
Oliver: You were what?
Stan: A dog bit me.
Oliver: I can't understand you. Spell it!
Stan: A dog bit me. B-i-*it*-me, bit me. And they took me to the hospital. The doctor said I might get hydrophosphates!
Oliver: Hydrophosphates... You mean hydrophobia! Come on over, I want to see you. And make it snappy!

Stan cannot understand Oliver's consternation. Oliver looks at the camera, as if to say: 'How can anyone be so stupid?' He shows Stan his wedding photo (Blanche Payson is his unattractive bride) and says: 'You never met my wife, did you? Stan replies: 'Yes, I never did!'

The two men cheerfully set about their task. At the end of the film the living-room and the kitchen, in fact the whole house, is a demolition case. The roof has come off, the walls have partly collapsed, and the whole place looks as though the proverbial bomb has hit it. Oliver is sitting wearing a fancy uniform, a Napoleonic three-cornered hat, and he has a black eye. He looks sadly around him. Stan asks him if there is anything else he can do. 'You've done quite enough already,' says Oliver, with no trace of sadness in his voice. 'Well, I'll be seeing you,' says Stan in a friendly tone. As he walks off, Oliver calls after him: 'Hey,

The Flying Deuces, (1939): Their first film for anyone other than Hal Roach was a feature made for RKO.

would you mind closing the door? I'd like to be alone.' The door and its frame are the only thing left standing: the wall they were situated in has been demolished. Stan shuts the door. We see Oliver Hardy sitting in the open air in the remains of his villa; there is a clap of thunder and a huge storm breaks out.

According to the articles and books that have been written about Laurel and Hardy, many of the presidents and crowned heads of the world have been admirers of the duo: they seem to have functioned as the nearest thing to a court jester to leaders such as Stalin, Tito, Churchill and Hirohito. Their 1931 short comedy feature, *Pardon Us*, was a film which particularly attracted the attention of the helmsmen of many ships of state. The film was distributed in French-, Spanish-, Italian- and German-language versions. Some of Hal Roach's most experienced people worked on the film: James Parrott directed, George Stevens in charge of the cameras, editor Richard Currier sat behind the Moviola, the scripts were by H.M. Walker and the film included superb performances by Wilfred Lucas as the prison governor, Stanley Sandford as a warder, Otto Fries as the prison dentist and Charlie Hall as his assistant, James Finlayson as the prison teacher and Walter Long as the prisoner they call Tiger. All Roach's best-known actors appear as well, including Roach himself and James Parrott. The watchword of the film, stated in the titles at the beginning, is: 'Mr Hardy is a man of wonderful ideas – so is Mr Laurel, as long as he doesn't try to think.'

Laurel and Hardy try their hands at selling bootleg liquor during Prohibition. Stan offers the business to a policeman in the belief that he is a tram conductor. When they are being registered on their arrival in prison, the governor says: 'If you are good prisoners, everything will be okay. If you are not, if you break the rules, then it will be just plain hell on earth! Now, do you understand?'

This first Laurel and Hardy feature film (though it was only fifty-six minutes long) shows a prison whose workings are likely to have a powerfully deterrent effect. The scenes could almost come from Fritz Lang's *Metropolis:* to use the words of the governor, the prison is just 'plain hell on earth'. So it is no surprise that there is a revolt led by (if his appearance is anything to go by) the world's most vicious and deranged criminal, played by Walter Long. In the dining-room, a huge, grim hall where endless rows of men sitting at long tables are given bowls of soup made out of vegetable peelings, weapons are secretly handed out under the tables. Stan has a machine-gun pressed into his hands, and in his shock brings it above the table. Oliver gives a terrified scream, the weapon begins to chatter and the rebellion has begun, somewhat earlier than Walter Long had planned.

Naturally, Laurel and Hardy do everything wrong so that it looks as though they have actually been trying to put down the rebellion. As a gesture of thanks they are released from the prison. Back in civilian clothes, they stand in the warden's office to hear him give an exaggeratedly friendly farewell speech. 'Boys – and you *are* my boys, those warning shots you fired in the dining-hall saved us from a disaster

Helpmates, (1931).

of *cataclysmic* proportions! I want you to look upon these few months of your life as simply a *hiatus*! Begin life anew. Forget this. Let this episode here be just a *quietus* to be *obliterated* from your memory. Don't forget I'm your friend. Anything I can do to help you where you stopped off, let me know. Call me anytime.' Oliver Hardy nods in pleasure. Stan is obviously thinking – he is a bit worried by all the long words he doesn't understand. They are being offered help to return to the position they were in before they went to prison. Why not take the governor up on his offer? So Stan asks confidently: 'Can we take your order for a couple of cases?'

Pardon Us is one of the very best Laurel and Hardy features. The scenes in the dentist's waiting-room and later on in the surgery where Oliver goes in to offer Stan moral support (and where he ends up having a tooth brutally pulled instead of Stan) are amongst the greatest scenes in film comedy. Once they leave the prison they disguise themselves as negro cotton-pickers; Laurel and Hardy play this scene with consummate skill. Oliver sings 'Lazy Moon', his face blacked, and Stan dances gracefully as he sings. Compared to a tragedy, a comedy can sometimes give a more realistic view of real life. In *Pardon Us*, two fugitives living from day to day show us just how true this can be. And when they do, it makes us laugh.

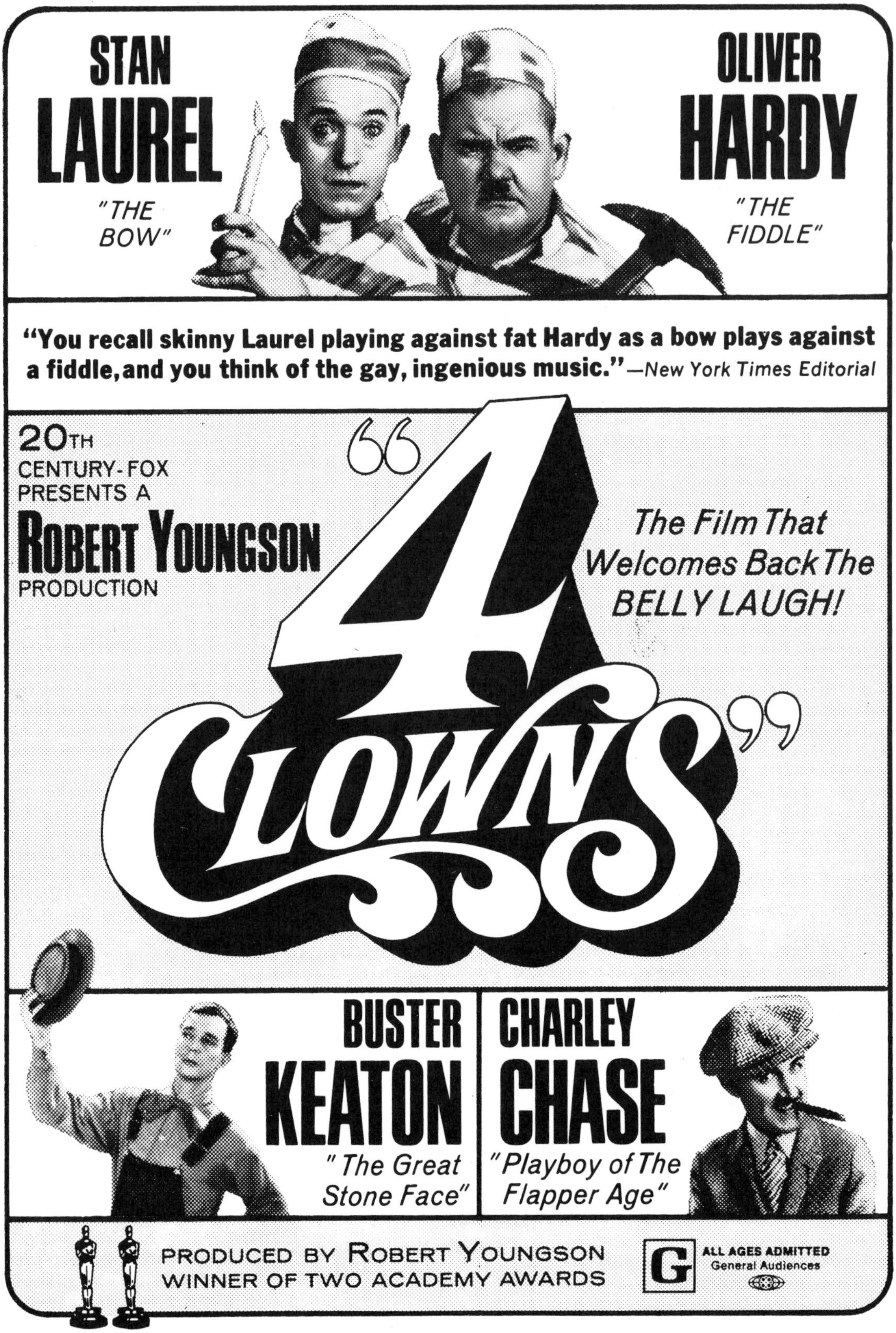
STAN LAUREL
"THE BOW"
OLIVER HARDY
"THE FIDDLE"
"You recall skinny Laurel playing against fat Hardy as a bow plays against a fiddle, and you think of the gay, ingenious music." —New York Times Editorial
20TH CENTURY-FOX PRESENTS A
ROBERT YOUNGSON PRODUCTION
"4 CLOWNS"
The Film That Welcomes Back The BELLY LAUGH!
BUSTER KEATON
"The Great Stone Face"
CHARLEY CHASE
"Playboy of The Flapper Age"
PRODUCED BY ROBERT YOUNGSON
WINNER OF TWO ACADEMY AWARDS
G
ALL AGES ADMITTED
General Audiences

10

Compilations

In 1948, Hal Roach Senior sold the negatives and the rights to a large number of his sound shorts to an American distributor with the ambitious name of Film Classics. The company specialized in old black-and-white films, its customers including film clubs, universities, art houses and individual film enthusiasts with a particular love of the comedy classics.

Film Classics did not make as much of a success of this important task as they might have done. In fact, they went at it like a bull in a china shop. The original opening credits were cut out remorsely despite the fact that their lettering and design made them an integral part of the film's whole nostalgic appeal, and the MGM lion gave way to the well-known marble plaque (sometimes at the beginning of the Film Classics versions of Laurel and Hardy we hear the lion roaring, but we do not see it).

Regal Films in the United States made changes which were just as drastic. This was the company that bought the rights to Hal Roach's Laurel and Hardy features to be made into television series. They too set about the films with the scissors and turned them into 'short comedies' cut to the right length for TV showing, again provided with new titles. Once this had happened, generations of TV viewers grew up watching these chopped-up Laurel and Hardy films, not knowing which films the succession of scenes they watched originally came from. The pseudo-two-reelers became known by the titles their new distributor had given them, and it is often the case that a film in one of the TV listings magazines has a title which cannot be traced back to the original Laurel and Hardy filmography: nine times out of ten, it is 1950s versions we are watching whenever a Laurel and Hardy film is shown on TV in England, America or Canada.

To show the scale of the problem, here is a partial list of titles: first, the name under which the 'new' films are currently distributed, and then the original films they were distilled from.

New Title	*Original Title*
Alpine Antics	Swiss Miss
Alter Ego	A Chump at Oxford
All Wet	Bonnie Scotland
Bang Bang	Bonnie Scotland
Cry Babies	The Devil's Brother (Fra Diavolo)
A Day at the Studio	Pick a Star
Do it Yourself	Blockheads
Doughboy Daze	Pack up your Troubles
Easy Come, Easy Go	The Devil's Brother (Fra Diavolo)
Gyp the Gypsies	Bohemian Girl
Horn Hero	Saps at Sea
In a Mess	Bonnie Scotland
In Trouble	The Devil's Brother (Fra Diavolo)
Kidnapped	Bonnie Scotland
Melody on the Move	Swiss Miss
No Flies on Us	Flying Deuces
Smitherines	Pack up your Troubles
The Rookies	Bonnie Scotland
Twin Trouble	Our Relations
Wacky Westerners	Way out West
Whatta Stir	Pardon Us
Where Now	Saps at Sea

Double Whoopee, (1929): Laurel and Hardy as hotel porters, with Jean Harlow, whose dress has got caught in the door of the taxi.

Me and My Pal, (1933): The pair grapple with a jigsaw puzzle for long minutes in front of a motionless camera.

Since 1968, cinemas and television stations have been showing MGM's eighty-four-minute 'feature film', *The Best of Laurel and Hardy.* This is made up of extracts from Hal Roach comedies re-edited and re-titled by James L. Woolcott. Again, the new name is followed by the original title.

New Title	*Original Title*
Crime and Punishment	Pardon Us
A Dollar a Head	The Live Ghost
Double Trouble	Our Relations
How to Visit a Sick Friend	County Hospital
Moonlight and Romance	Our Wife
Music Hath Charms	Below Zero
Night Owls and Alley Cats	Night Owls
The $125 Misunderstanding	One Good Turn
Tallyho!	Be Big
Three's a Crowd	Their First Mistake

Some of the old two-reelers have also been placed together as 'new' feature films. For example, the three shorts *County Hospital* (1932;

Oliver Hardy leaves the hospital with his right leg in plaster), *Them Thar Hills* (1934; on their doctor's advice, Laurel and Hardy with his plaster cast go off to the hills) and *Tit for Tat* (1935; they find the same couple opposite them as in *Them Thar Hills* and Mae Busch actually refers to their earlier meeting) obviously lend themselves to being placed back-to-back as a feature film. And so they were, and the result was received enthusiastically by prewar audiences.

In 1957, Robert Youngson (1917-74) cashed in on the success which Laurel and Hardy's short films had experienced on television. He took extracts from silent comedies by Laurel and Hardy, Carole Lombard, Ben Turpin, Will Rogers and Harry Langdon and put them together as a seventy-eight-minute compilation to be shown in cinemas, called *The Golden Age of Comedy,* Again, this film was a great success. And indeed, the job of putting together clips to create a new product was in good hands: Youngson had received Academy Awards in 1951 and 1954 for his documentaries, *World of Kids* and *This Mechanical Age,* and had been nominated for Oscars in 1949, 1950 and 1955 for *Spills and Chills, Blaze Busters* and *Gadgets Galore.* He worked for Pathé News between 1941 and 1948, and then for Warner Brothers as a producer, writer and director until 1956.

The Golden Age of Comedy was the first of a series of eight compilations of material from mostly silent American comedies. Youngson brought fragments of films from the early years of cinematography to a much wider audience than hitherto. It is more than likely that many film-goers first became interested in such comedians as Laurel and Hardy, Charlie Chaplin, Buster Keaton, Harold Lloyd, Snub Pollard, Fatty Arbuckle, Harry Langdon, Ben Turpin, Monty Banks, Al St John, the Sennett Bathing Beauties and Cameo the Wonderdog after seeing one of Youngson's anthologies of all that was great in the cinema of comedy.

One by one, Youngson's compilations, full of high points from the history of film, drew crowds to the box offices, particularly in the United States. Their titles were: *When Comedy Was King* (1960), *Days of Thrills and Laughter* (1961), *Thirty Years of Fun* (1962), *MGM's Big Parade of Laughs* (1964), *Laurel and Hardy's Laughing Twenties* (1965), *The Further Perils of Laurel and Hardy* (1967) and *The Four Clowns* (1970). The four clowns in the latter film were Charley Chase, Buster Keaton and Laurel and Hardy. Youngson took great care in copying the old films; his scripts are informative and the clips well-chosen.

Unlike Robert Youngson, Jay Ward used both silents and talkies for his 1965 compilation, *The Crazy World of Laurel and Hardy.* Radio and television comedian Garry Moore wrote the scripts and it is his voice we hear introducing the clips: at the end, as Stan and Oliver do a little dance in front of Fin's saloon, he says: 'Mr Laurel and Mr Hardy. Two gentle gentlemen.' Again, this is an excellent compilation, though some scenes have passed almost before the eye has registered them. But it also includes longer scenes from *Going Bye Bye* (1934), *Bacon*

Grabbers (1929), *Towed in a Hole* (1932, *Laurel and Hardy: fresh fish, crabs a speciality*), *Swiss Miss* (1938, Stan, wearing a Tyrolean suit, plucks a chicken and uses the feathers to make a snowstorm so that he can get close to a St Bernard and steal the contents of the barrel round its neck), *Way Out West* (1937), *The Music Box* (1932), *Busy Bodies* (1933) and a number of other films. The film critic in the *New York Times* began his review of *The Crazy World of Laurel and Hardy*: 'How to make money without actually filming anything.'

Apart from the making of compilations of their work, one other phenomenon surrounding Laurel and Hardy's films is of note. This is Colorization, a trademark belonging to Hal Roach Studios in Los Angeles. It is unclear whether this company arose from the original Hal Roach Studios or had historical ties with it. Did Hal Roach Sr ever sanction the idea? It is possible, but either way, the new Roach company uses computers in an attempt to add a new dimension to Laurel and Hardy shorts by adding colour to them. According to *TV World* (March 1985), which devoted an article to the subject, entitled 'Coloring Magic', the results are good to very good. Vidcolor Image, a Canadian company, also specializes in adding colour to black-and-white films electronically. Hal Roach Sr elected to stay with monochromatic film for reasons of economy at the end of the 1930s,

Their Purple Moment, (1928).

after colour had been on the scene for some time. As long as the chances of colour Laurel and Hardy films being shown on TV are increasing, no one can object to this ingenious and painstaking process. After all, every colour TV set has a button which will instantly render the image black-and-white again.

Way Out West, (1936).

FILMOGRAPHY

The films of Stan Laurel

1917
Nuts in May
The Evolution of Fashion
Lucky Dog

1918
Hickory Hiram
Phoney Photos
Whose Zoo
No Place Like Jail
Huns and Hyphens
Just Rambling Along
Bears and Bad Men
Frauds and Frenzies
It's Great to be Crazy

1919
Do You Love Your Wife?
Hustling for Health
Hoot Man (also: Hoot Mon!)

1921
The Egg
The Weak-End Party
Mud and Sand
The Pest

1923
When Knights Were Cold
The Handy Man
Noon Whistle
White Wings
Under Two Jags
Pick and Shovel
Collars and Cuffs
Kill or Cure
Gags and Air
Oranges and Lemons
Short Orders
A Man About Town
Roughest Africa
Frozen Hearts
The Whole Truth
Save the Ship
The Soilers
Scorching Sands
Mother's Joy

1924
Smithy
Postage Due
Zeb vs. Paprika
Brothers under the Chin
Near Dublin
Rupert of Hee-Haw
Wide Open Spaces
Short Kilts
Mixed Nuts
Madam Mix-Up (also: Mandarin Mix-Up)
Detained
Monsieur Don't Care
West of Hot Dog

1925
Somewhere in Wrong
Twins
Pie-Eyed
Snow Hawk
Navy Blue Days
The Sleuth
Yes, Yes Nanette (director)
Dr Pyckle and Mr Pride
Half a Man
Unfriendly Enemies (director)
Moonlight and Noses (director)
Wandering Papas (director)

1926
Enough to Do (director)
Madame Mysterie (director)
Never too Old (director)
The Merry Widower (director)
Wise Guys Prefer Brunettes (director) (also: Why Guys Prefer Brunettes)
Atta Boy
Get 'Em Young
Raggedy Rose
On the Front Page

1927
Seeing the World
Eve's Love Letters
Now I'll Tell One

1928
Should Tall Men Marry?

The films of Oliver Hardy

1914
Outwitting Dad
Back to the Farm
Pins Are Lucky
The Soubrette and the Simp
The Smuggler's Daughter
The Female Cop

1915
What He Forgot
Cupid's Target
Spaghetti and Lottery
Gus and the Anarchists
Shoddy the Tailor
The Paper Hanger's Helper
Spaghetti à la Mode
Charley's Aunt
Artists and Models
The Tramps
Prize Baby
An Expensive Visit
Cleaning Time
Mixed Flats
Safety Worst
Twin Sisters
Baby
Who Stole the Doggies?
A Lucky Strike
The New Butler
Matilda's Legacy
Her Choice
The Cannibal King
What a Cinch!
Clothes Make the Man
The Dead Letter
Avenging Bill
The Haunted Hat
The Simp and the Sophomores
Babe's School Days
Ethel's Romeos
A Bungalow Bungle
Three Rings and a Goat
A Rheumatic Joint
Something in her Eye
A Janitor's Joyful Job
Fatty's Fatal Fun
Ups and Downs

1916
This Way Out
Chickens
A Frenzied Finance
Busted Hearts
A Stickey Affair
Bungles' Rainy Day
The Try-out
One Two Many
Bungles Enforces the Law

The Serenade
Bungles' Elopement
Nerve and Gasoline
Bungles Lands a Job
Their Vacation
Mama's Boys
A Battle Royal
All for a Girl
Hired and Fired
What's Sauce for the Goose
The Brave Ones
The Water Cure
30 Days
Baby Doll
The Schemers
Sea Dogs
Hungry Hearts
Edison Bugg's Invention
Never Again
Better Halves
A Day at School
A Terrible Tragedy
Spaghetti
Aunt Bill
The Heroes
It Happened in Pikersville
Human Hounds
Dreamy Knights
Life Savers
Their Honeymoon
An Aerial Joyride
Side-Tracked
Stranded
Love and Duty
Artistic Atmosphere
The Reformer
Royal Blood
The Candy Trial
A Precious Parcel
A Maid to Order
Twin Flats
A Warm Reception
Pipe Dreams
Mother's Child
Prize Winners
Ambitious Ethel
The Guilty One
He Winked and Won
Fat and Fickle

1917
Boycotted Baby
Wanted – A Bad Man
The Other Girl
The Love Bugs
Lucky Dog
Back Stage
The Hero
Dough-Nuts
Cupid's Rival
The Villain
The Millionaire
A Mix-Up in Hearts
The Goat
The Genius
The Stranger
The Fly Cop
The Modiste
The Star Boarder
The Chief Cook
The Candy Kid
The Station Master
The Hobo
The Pest
The Prospector

1918
The Bandmaster
The Slave
The Artist
The Barber
King Solomon
The Orderly
His Day Out
The Rogue
The Scholar
The Messenger
The Handy Man
Bright and Early
The Straight and Narrow
Playmates

1919
Freckled Fish
Hop the Bellhop
Lions and Ladies
Mules and Mortgages
Tootsies and Tamales
Healthy and Happy

Flips and Flops
Yaps and Yokels
Mates and Models
Squabs and Squabbles
Bungs and Bunglers

1920
Switches and Sweeties
Dames and Dentists
Maid and Muslin
Squeaks and Squawks
Fists and Fodder
Pals and Pugs
He Laughs Last
Springtime
The Decorator
His Jonah Day
The Back Yard

1921
The Nuisance
The Blizzard
The Tourist
The Fall Guy

1922
The Sawmill
Golf
Fortune's Mask
The Little Wildcat
The Counter Jumper

1923
One Stolen Night
Three Ages

1924
The King of Wild Horses
The Girl in the Limousine
Her Boy Friend
Kid Speed

1925
Is Marriage the Bunk?
Stick Around
Hop To It!
The Wizard of Oz
Isn't Life Terrible?
Yes, Yes, Nanette
Enough To Do
Could Sailors Marry?
The Perfect Clown

1926
Stop Look and Listen
A Bankrupt Honeymoon
Madame Mystery
Say it with Babies
Long Fliv the King
Gentle Cyclone
Thundering Fleas
A Sea Dog's Tale
Along Came Auntie
Crazy Like a Fox
Bromo and Juliet
Be Your Age
The Nickle Hopper

1927
Should Men Walk Home?
Why Girls Say No
The Honorable
Mr. Buggs
No Man's Law
Crazy to Act
Fluttering Hearts
The Lighter That Failed
Love 'Em and Feed 'Em
Assistant Wives

1928
Galloping Ghosts
Barnum and Ringling Inc.

1939
Zenobia

1950
The Fighting Kentuckian
Riding High

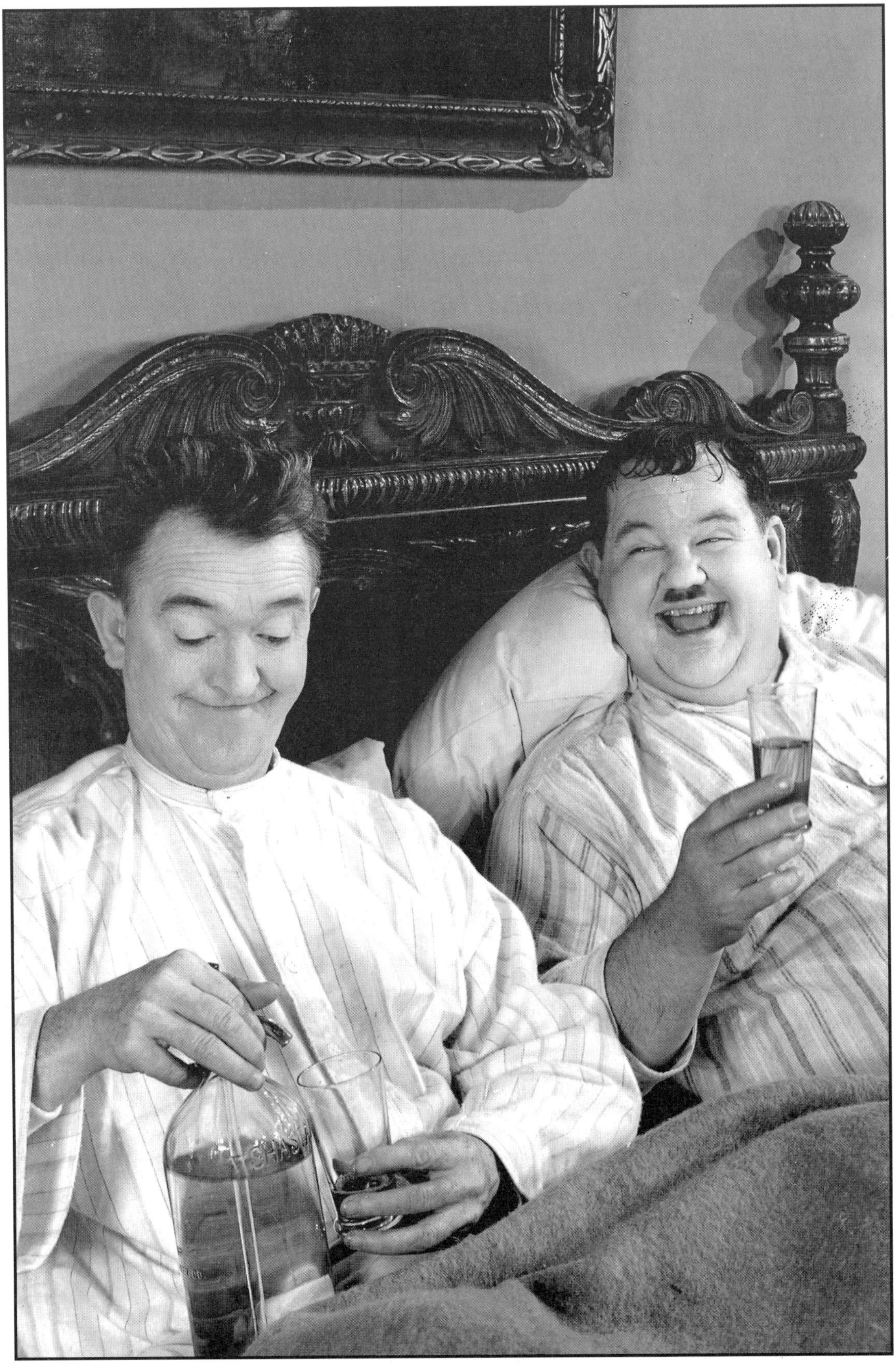

The films of Stan Laurel and Oliver Hardy

Lucky Dog
1917, one reel, Anderson/Metro
director: Jesse Robbins, camera: unknown

45 Minutes from Hollywood
1926, two reels, Roach/Pathé
director: Fred L. Guiol, camera: unknown

Duck Soup
1927, two reels, Roach/Pathé
director: Fred L. Guiol, camera: unknown

Slipping Wives
1927, two reels, Roach/Pathé
director: Fred L. Guiol, camera: George Stevens

Love 'Em and Weep
1927, two reels, Roach/Pathé
director: Fred L. Guiol, camera: unknown

Why Girls Love Sailors
1927, two reels, Roach/Pathé
director: Fred L. Guiol, camera: unknown

With Love and Hisses
1927, two reels, Roach/Pathé
director: Fred L. Guiol, camera: unknown

Hats Off (1927): Laurel and Hardy as door-to-door washing-machine salesmen who carry their wares with them, after a hat fight.

Sugar Daddies
1927, two reels, Roach/MGM
director: Fred L. Guiol, camera: George Stevens

Sailors Beware
1927, two reels, Roach/Pathé
director: Hal Yates, camera: unknown

The Second Hundred Years
1927, two reels, Roach/MGM
director: Fred L. Guiol, camera: unknown

Call of the Cuckoos
1927, two reels, Roach/MGM
director: Clyde A. Bruckman and Leo McCarey, camera: Floyd Jackman

Hats Off
1927, two reels, Roach/MGM
director: Hal Yates and Leo McCarey, camera: unknown

Do Detectives Think?
1927, two reels, Roach/Pathé
director: Fred L. Guiol, camera: unknown

Putting Pants on Philip
1927, two reels, Roach/MGM
director: Clyde A. Bruckman and Leo McCarey, camera: George Stevens

The Battle of the Century
1927, two reels, Roach/MGM
director: Clyde A. Bruckman and Leo McCarey, camera: George Stevens

Leave 'Em Laughing
1928 two reels, Roach/MGM
director: Clyde A. Bruckman and Leo McCarey, camera: George Stevens

Flying Elephants
1928, two reels, Roach/Pathé
director: Frank Butler, camera: unkown

The Finishing Touch
1928, two reels, Roach/MGM
director: Clyde A. Bruckman and Leo McCarey, camera: George Stevens

From Soup to Nuts
1928, two reels, Roach/MGM
director: Edgar Livingston Kennedy and Leo McCarey, camera: Len Powers

You're Darn Tootin'
1928, two reels, Roach/MGM
director: Edgar Livingston Kennedy and Leo McCarey, camera: Floyd Jackman

Their Purple Moment
1928, two reels, Roach/MGM
director: James Parrott and Leo McCarey, camera: George Stevens

Should Married Men Go Home
1928, two reels, Roach/MGM
director: James Parrott and Leo McCarey, camera: George Stevens

From Soup to Nuts (1928): the first film in which the duo were credited.

Early to Bed
1928, two reels, Roach/MGM
director: Emmett Flynn and Leo McCarey, camera: George Stevens

Two Tars
1928, two reels, Roach/MGM
director: James Parrott and Leo McCarey, camera: George Stevens

Habeas Corpus
1928, two reels, Roach/MGM
director: James Parrott and Leo McCarey, camera: Len Powers

We Faw Down
1928, two reels, Roach/MGM
director: Leo McCarey, camera: unknown

Liberty
1929, two reels, Roach/MGM
director: Leo McCarey, camera: George Stevens

Wrong Again
1929, two reels, Roach/MGM
director: Leo McCarey, camera: George Stevens and Jack Roach

The Hoose-Gow (1929): Stan and Oliver are released from prison.

That's My Wife
1929, two reels, Roach/MGM
director: Lloyd French and Leo McCarey, camera: unknown

Big Business
1929, two reels, Roach/MGM
director: James W. Thorne and Leo McCarey, camera: George Stevens

Unaccustomed As We Are
1929, two reels, Roach/MGM
director: Lewis R. Foster, camera: unknown

Double Whoopee
1929, two reels, Roach/MGM
director: Lewis R. Foster, camera: George Stevens

Berth Marks
1929, two reels, Roach/MGM
director: Lewis R. Foster, camera: Len Powers

Men O'War
1929, two reels, Roach/MGM
director: Lewis R. Foster, camera: George Stevens and Jack Roach

Perfect Day
1929, two reels, Roach/MGM
director: James Parrott, camera: unknown

They Go Boom
1929, two reels, Roach/MGM
director: James Parrott, camera: unknown

Bacon Grabbers
1929, two reels, Roach/MGM
director: Lewis R. Foster, camera: George Stevens

The Hoose-Gow
1929, two reels, Roach/MGM
director: James Parrott, camera: George Stevens and Len Powers

The Hollywood Revue of 1929
1929, 82 minutes, MGM
director: Charles F. Riesner, camera: John Arnold *et al.*
In this film Stan Laurel and Oliver Hardy appear as jugglers.

Angora Love
1929, two reels, Roach/MGM
director: Lewis R. Foster, camera: George Stevens

Angora Love (1929): with Edgar Kennedy.

Night Owls
1930, two reels, Roach/MGM
director: James Parrott, camera: George Stevens

Blotto
1930, two reels, Roach/MGM
director: James Parrott, camera: George Stevens

Brats
1930, two reels, Roach/MGM
director: James Parrott, camera: George Stevens

Below Zero
1930, two reels, Roach/MGM
director: James Parrott, camera: George Stevens

The Rogue Song
1930, 115 minutes, MGM
director: Lionel Barrymore, camera: Percy Hilburn and Edgar Schoenbaum
Stan as Ali-Bek, Oliver as Murza-Bek

Hog Wild
1930, two reels, Roach/MGM
director: James Parrott, camera: George Stevens

The Laurel and Hardy Murder Case
1930, two reels, Roach/MGM
director: James Parrott, camera: Walter Lundin and George Stevens

Another Fine Mess
1930, two reels, Roach/MGM
director: James Parrott, camera: George Stevens

Be Big
1931, two reels, Roach/MGM
director: James Parrott, camera: Art Lloyd

Chickens Come Home
1931, two reels, Roach/MGM
director: James W. Horne, camera: Art Lloyd and Jack Stevens

The Stolen Jools
1931, two reels, National Screen Service/Paramount
director: William McGann, camera: unknown
Laurel and Hardy play police patrolmen in a National Vaudeville Association film to benefit tuberculosis research.

Laughing Gravy
1931, two reels, Roach/MGM
director: James W. Horne, camera: Art Lloyd

Blotto (1930): Laurel and Hardy drunk in a nightclub.

Our Wife
1931, two reels, Roach/MGM
director: James W. Horne, camera: Art Lloyd

Pardon Us
1931, 56 minutes, Roach/MGM
director: James Parrott, camera: George Stevens, dialogue: Hiram Walker

Come Clean
1931, two reels, Roach/MGM
director: James W. Horne, camera: Art Lloyd

One Good Turn
1931, two reels, Roach/MGM
director: James W. Horne, camera: Art Lloyd

Beau Hunks
1931, four reels, Roach/MGM
director: James W. Horne, camera: Art Lloyd and Jack Stevens

On the Loose
1931, two reels, Roach/MGM
director: Hal E. Roach, camera: Len Powers
Guest appearance by Laurel and Hardy in Thelma Todd/Zasu Pitts short.

Beau Hunks (1931): their second feature film.

Any Old Port (1932).

Helpmates
1932, two reels, Roach/MGM
director: James Parrott, camera: Art Lloyd

Any Old Port
1932, two reels, Roach/MGM
director: James W. Horne, camera: Art Lloyd

The Music Box
1932, three reels, Roach/MGM
director: James Parrott, camera: Walter Lundin and Len Powers

The Chimp
1932, three reels, Roach/MGM
director: James Parrott, camera: Walter Lundin

County Hospital
1932, two reels, Roach/MGM
director: James Parrott, camera: Art Lloyd

Scram!
1932, two reels, Roach/MGM
director: Raymond McCarey, camera: Art Lloyd

Pack Up Your Troubles
1932, 68 minutes, Roach/MGM
director: George Marshall and Raymond McCarey, camera: Art Lloyd
dialogue: Hiram Walker

Their First Mistake
1932, two reels, Roach/MGM
director: George Marshall, camera: unknown

Towed in a Hole
1932, two reels, Roach/MGM
director: George Marshall, camera: Art Lloyd

Twice Two
1933, two reels, Roach/MGM
director: James Parrott, camera: Art Lloyd

Their First Mistake (1932).

Me and My Pal
1933, two reels, Roach/MGM
director: Charles Rogers, camera: Art Lloyd

Fra Diavolo (The Devil's Brother)
1933, 90 minutes, Roach/MGM
director: Hal E. Roach and Charles Rogers, camera: Art Lloyd and Hap Depew

The Midnight Patrol
1933, two reels, Roach/MGM
director: Lloyd French, camera: Art Lloyd

Busy Bodies
1933, two reels, Roach/MGM
director: Lloyd French, camera: Art Lloyd

Wild Poses
1933, two reels, Roach/MGM
director: Robert McGowan, camera: Francis Corby
Guest appearance by Laurel and Hardy as two babies in an 'Our Gang' comedy.

Dirty Work
1933, two reels, Roach/MGM
director: Lloyd French, camera: Kenneth Peach

Sons of the Desert
1933, 68 minutes, Roach/MGM
director: William A. Steiner, camera: Kenneth Peach

Oliver the Eighth
1934, three reels, Roach/MGM
director: Lloyd French, camera: Art Lloyd

The Hollywood Party
1934, 68 minutes, MGM
director: Richard Boleslavky, Allan Dwan and Roy Rowland, camera: James Wong Howe
Guest appearance by Laurel and Hardy.

Going Bye Bye
1934, two reels, Roach/MGM
director: Charles Rogers, camera: Francis Corby

Them Thar Hills
1934, two reels, Roach/MGM
director: Charles Rogers, camera: Art Lloyd

Babes in Toyland
1934, 79 minutes, Roach/MGM
director: Charles Rogers and Gus Meins, camera: Art Lloyd and Francis Corby

The Live Ghost
1934, two reels, Roach/MGM
director: Charles Rogers, camera: Art Lloyd

Tit for Tat
1935, two reels, Roach/MGM
director: Charles Rogers, camera: Art Lloyd

The Fixer Uppers
1935, two reels, Roach/MGM
director: Charles Rogers, camera: Art Lloyd

Thicker Than Water
1935, two reels, Roach/MGM
director: James W. Horne, camera: Art Lloyd

Bonnie Scotland
1935, 80 minutes, Roach/MGM
director: James W. Horne, camera: Art Lloyd and Walter Lundin

You're Darn Tootin (1928).

The Bohemian Girl
1936, 70 minutes, Roach/MGM
director: James W. Horne and Charles Rogers, camera: Art Lloyd and Francis Corby

On the Wrong Trek
1936, two reels, Roach/MGM
director: Charles Parrott and Harold Law, camera: Art Lloyd
Guest appearance by Laurel and Hardy as roadside hitchhikers in a Charley Chase comedy.

Our Relations
1936, 74 minutes, Roach/MGM
director: Harry Lachman, camera: Rudolph Maté

Way Out West
1937, 65 minutes, Roach/MGM
director: James W. Horne, camera: Art Lloyd and Walter Lundin

Pick A Star
1937, 70 minutes, Roach/MGM
director: Edward Sedgwick, camera: Norbert Brodine
Guest appearance by Laurel and Hardy in a remake of the 1930 MGM feature film, *Free and Easy.*

A Haunting We Will Go (1942), the second feature Laurel and Hardy made for 20th Century-Fox.

The Bullfighters (1945): a sad film, for it shows Laurel and Hardy's fortunes on the wane.

Swiss Miss
1938, 72 minutes, Roach/MGM
director: John G. Blystone, camera: Art Lloyd and Norbert Brodine

Blockheads
1939, 58 minutes, Roach/MGM
director: John G. Blystone, camera: Art Lloyd

The Flying Deuces
1939, 69 minutes, Morros/RKO
director: A. Edward Sutherland, camera: Art Lloyd and Elmer Dyer

A Chump at Oxford
1940, 42 minutes, (USA), 63 minutes (Europe), Roach/UA
director: Alfred Goulding, camera: Art Lloyd

Saps at Sea
1940, 57 minutes Roach/UA
director: Gordon Douglas, camera: Art Lloyd

Great Guns
1941, 74 minutes, 20th Century-Fox
director: Monty Banks, camera: Glen McWilliams

A-Haunting We Will Go
1942, 67 minutes, 20th Century-Fox
director: Alfred Werker, camera: Glen McWilliams

The Tree in a Testtube
1943, one reel, 20th Century-Fox
director: Charles McDonald, camera: A.H.C. Sintzenich (in 16mm Kodachrome)
Part of a series 'US Government Defense Reel' about the use of wood in wartime.

Air Raid Wardens
1947, 67 minutes, MGM
director: Edward Sedgwick, camera: Walter Lundin

Jitterbugs
1943, 74 minutes, 20th Century-Fox
director: Malcolm St Clair, camera: Lucien Andriot

The Dancing Masters
1943, 63 minutes, 20th Century-Fox
director: Malcolm St Clair, camera: Norbert Brodine

The Big Noise
1944, 74 minutes, 20th Century-Fox
director: Malcolm St Clair, camera: Joe McDonald

The Bullfighters
1945, 69 minutes, 20th Century-Fox
director: Malcolm St. Clair, camera: Norbert Brodine

Nothing But Trouble
1945, 70 minutes, MGM
director: Sam Taylor, camera: Charles Salerno

Atoll K
1950, 82 minutes (USA), 98 minutes (Europe), Sirius/Fortezza
director: Leo Joannon and John Berry, camera: Armand Thirard

Acknowledgements

All the stills used in this book are from the author's own collection. Copyright belongs to Hal Roach Studios Inc., American Broadcasting Company, Columbia Broadcasting System Inc., Columbia Pictures Corporation, Metro-Goldwyn-Mayer, Inc., National Broadcasting Company, Inc., Paramount Pictures Corporation, RKO Radio Pictures, 20th Century-Fox Corporation, United Artists Corporation, Universal Pictures Company and Toho International.

A word of personal thanks is due to André J. Dresscher, Robert A. Fuller, Wim and Jef Hartsuyker, Piet Hartog, Bram Reijnhoudt, Joop P. Smits, Piet Spek, Tjitte de Vries and the late F. Lettinga and Lex Werkheim.

Analysing film by watching it in the cinema is a well-nigh impossible task. A cinema showing cannot simply be stopped whenever required: the show must go on. The writer on cinema can only control things when the film is taken out of its cinema context and he can use a video, editing table or his own projector. Then you can look at specific parts of a film, watch them several times if need be, and form a judgement of the film as a whole. You can take a closer look at things like camera angles, and listen to the script and the music independently of the moving image. Now that films originally produced for a cinema audience can be viewed in the privacy of one's own home, anyone can sit there and watch a film from an analytical point of view: a luxury which was hitherto the preserve of a select band of film critics with access to the necessary equipment.

Many of the scenes from films described in this book could only be recounted on paper with the aid of the author's collection of 16mm films. I also used a 35mm editing table and a video recorder, which enabled me to watch films frame by frame and even back to front. Things have come a long way over the last two decades, when most ordinary people could only write about a film from memory, perhaps with the aid of a few notes scribbled in the darkness of the cinema.

Not that this book is faultless, of course: it makes no claim to being comprehensive, and indeed it is difficult to be comprehensive on a subject like Laurel and Hardy. Aside from a large number of oral sources, it is mainly the original versions of their films, produced by Hal Roach, that I have used as my reference material.

Bibliography

King of Comedy
Mack Sennett and Cameron Shipp
Pinnacle Books, New York, 1954

W. C. Fields: His Follies and Fortunes
Robert Lewis Taylor
Doubleday & Company, Garden City, 1949

The Entertainers
Pitman House, London, 1980

Konstanten in de komedie
H. van den Bergh
Moussault, Amsterdam, 1972

Mr Laurel & Mr Hardy
John McCabe
Robson Books, London, 1976

Music for the Movies
Tony Thomas
Barnes & Co., Cranbury, 1973

Nieuw Weekblad voor de Cinematografie
's-Gravenhage, 1930–40, 1945–50

From Chaplin to Allen
Roxanne Howard
Nostalgia Press, New York, 1980

Stan
Fred Lawrence Guiles
Michael Joseph, London, 1980

Whatever Became Of...?
Richard Lampinsky
ACE Books, New York City, 1968

Starring Robert Benchley
Robert Redding
University of New Mexico Press, Albuquerque, 1973

Every Day's a Matinee
Max Wilk
W.W. Norton & Company, New York, 1975

The Golden Age of Television
Max Wilk
Dell Publishing, New York, 1976

Comedy Films 1894-1954
John Montgomery
George Allen & Unwin, London, 1968

Kings of the B's
Todd McCarthy and Charles Flynn
Irwin & Company, Toronto, 1975

Growing Up in Hollywood
Robert Parrish
Harvest HBJ, New York, 1976

The Funsters
James Robert Parrish and William T. Leonard
Arlington House, New Rochelle, 1979

The Public is Never Wrong
Adolphe Zukor and Dale Kramer
G.P. Putman's Sons, New York City, 1953

The Movie Moguls
Philip French
Weidenfeld & Nicolson, London, 1969

All the Stars in Heaven
Gary Carey
Robson Books, London, 1982

Index